LOVE TRANCES

HOW TO HYPNOTIZE MEN TO LOVE YOU AND DO YOUR BIDDING

By

Craig Rovinsky

This book is a work of non-fiction. Names and places have been changed to protect the privacy of all individuals. The events and situations are true.

© 2003 by Craig Rovinsky. All rights reserved.

No part of this book may be reproduced, stored in a retrieval system, or transmitted by any means, electronic, mechanical, photocopying, recording, or otherwise, without written permission from the author.

ISBN: 1-4107-1523-X (Paperback)
ISBN: 1-4107-4253-9 (Dust Jacket)

This book is printed on acid free paper.

1stBooks - rev. 03/25/03

Special thanks to my mother, Sarah, and John Ivan-Palmer.

A personal thank-you to the thousands of women over the years who have shared your lives and loves over a palm reading. It is the adventure of your lives that created Love Trances.

iv

to Sherry Ann

vi

Table of Contents

The Magic of Covert Hypnotism 1

What is Hypnotic Trance? 11

Basic Conversational Hypnosis 101 25

Conversation 102 Advanced Techniques 41

Love Trances From His Childhood 57

Hypnotic Keys to Unlock His Heart 69

Unmet Needs 83

Naturally Occurring Trances 97

Trance Magnifiers 111

A Ph.D. in Loveology 127

Some Very Common Situations 143

The Alpha Male Trance 155

Super Self-Hypnosis 163

Useful Hallucinations 175

viii

LOVE TRANCES

The Magic of Covert Hypnotism

Once upon a time a woman came to a palm reader. He gazed deeply into her hand and began, "You are now becoming the romance heroine you've always dreamed you could be..."

Are you tired of settling for what comes along in love? Are you ready to learn something new, willing to give yourself that chance?

One good husband is worth two good wives, for the scarcer things are the more they're valued.
Benjamin Franklin

Based on the thousands of women I've spoken with, it seems that about one in five men are good relationship material to begin with. Three in five can be made into relationship material if you know what you are doing, and one in five just don't have the emotional depth to form relationships. You also have quite a bit of competition out there from other women.

With the hypnotic skills you will learn in Love Trances you will have options on four of five eligible men, while other women will

Craig Rovinsky

have only a one in five chance and will have to rely on luck. You will also be able to weed out the hopeless ones fast so you don't waste your time on them. Love Trances is about taking control of your love life.

> The ability to teach a man to love you is often the difference between being lonely and being loved.

For years the best advertisers, salespeople, politicians, and preachers have used hypnosis to persuade you to buy their product or believe in their cause. They know what stage hypnotists know. Full hypnotic trance states can be obtained without a formal induction.

Though it is difficult to hypnotize someone against their will, it is very easy to do so without them being aware anything is happening.

Covert, conversational trance inductions are strong. These stage techniques are even more powerful in a one-on-one context. In Love Trances, I will share with you the

LOVE TRANCES

secrets I have learned in my twenty-five years as a hypnotist and palm reader.

I will teach you how to use my hypnotic techniques to create a magical bond between you and the man (or men) of your choice. You will learn how to evaluate a potential mate, and how to decide whether he is the type of man you wish to have a relationship with. Most important, you will learn how to create an intense love bond between yourself and him.

Told her I had always lived alone. And I probably always would. And all I wanted was my freedom. And she told me that she understood. But I let her do some of my laundry. And she slipped a few meals in between. The next thing I remember she was all moved in. And I was buying her a washing machine.
Jackson Browne

Love Trances grew from the combination of my experiences as a stage hypnotist and palm reader. As a stage hypnotist, I learned early on that trance is much easier to obtain than I ever expected. In my early years, I usually needed ten to fifteen minutes to complete hypnotic inductions on stage. The duration of the induction decreased as the years went by until sometimes I skipped the "induction" and just did the show.

Craig Rovinsky

I'm not the first hypnotist to notice this phenomenon. Kreskin and many others perform "no-induction" stage hypnotism shows. No matter what one calls it, rapid and deep trance can be easily obtained with what appears to be normal conversation.

> People recognize trance on stage but don't recognize it when it occurs in daily life.

Although stage hypnotism formed a basis for this work, being a palm reader is what made it all come together. More than 90% of my clients were women—nice, intelligent, attractive, sensual women, always with the same question. They can't find love, and wonder what they are doing wrong.

I would tell them what Benjamin Franklin said. It has really been true for hundreds of years—there just aren't enough good men out there. If you don't really know what you're doing, four of five men might be poor relationship material. Realizing that it really wasn't their fault reassured my clients, but I still believed that they deserved love.

A little at a time I began teaching my clients simple waking inductions they could use with potential and existing relationships. With early success came more experiments and ideas with the final judgment

LOVE TRANCES

determined by whether the induction worked.

After many years I found myself with piles of scribbled notes. Finally my wife (who has me thoroughly entranced) suggested that what I have could empower women romantically on a massive scale, that women could be the romance heroines in their own lives!

What is it about a romance novel heroine that makes her what you dream of being? She is strong, self-confident, and has the ability to tame a wild man to create love. She doesn't settle for whatever guy is available. Instead she screens potential romantic partners to see if they meet her standards. She is charismatic and hypnotic.

After finishing, you will have the tools to become the romance heroine in your own life.

An extremely effective technique is to study this with a girlfriend. This simple action will accelerate your learning rapidly.

What you should know is briefly summarized at the end of each chapter.

After the chapter summary you will find an assignment titled "Hypnotic Homework." Sometimes when reading a book there can be so much you don't know where to start.

Craig Rovinsky

The homework page will give you one task. Starting with this activity will allow you to easily begin making these new skills part of your life.

At the end of each chapter there is a page marked "HypnoJournal." These aren't just decoration. You will learn better and faster if you write down things, especially if you are designing trances for specific men. Write in the HypnoJournal pages anything that makes you think, anything you wonder about.

You will also notice that many of the examples are not specifically romance situations. You must think of this as a conversational approach.

> By practicing in daily life you will be automatic when you need to be.

Once you start to understand what you are doing things will become automatic, and not just in romantic situations. With your new communication tools you will become charismatic to most people you meet. It's a side effect of the practice. In Love Trances we will concentrate on creating love, but improving yourself this way will spill over to the rest of your life.

LOVE TRANCES

> After you have practiced Love Trances for a while it will begin to occur to you how personally powerful you really are. The inner confidence this gives you is priceless.

Every person has many individualized trance words that induce trance states, and numerous naturally occurring trance states. So sit back, relax, and open your mind to the idea that you can be powerful, sensual, and hypnotic. You can be the romance heroine in your own life. It's easy. Just take my hand and let's go to chapter two . . .

Craig Rovinsky

What You Should Know From This Chapter

Without something extra, only 1 in 5 men is good relationship material.

The ability to teach a man to love is often the difference between being lonely and being loved.

It is easy to hypnotize someone without their knowledge with seemingly normal conversation.

You can become the romance heroine in your own life by learning and using the tools of conversational hypnosis.

Use the notes pages for accelerated learning.

Have a study partner.

Try the Hypnotic Homework.

Hypnotic Homework

You will have days when you are charming, sexy, beautiful and totally irresistible. Still, despite everything, you are rejected. The result of this is although you know he is a blind moron rejection still has a sting.

LOVE TRANCES

What you need is some way to be happy when you want to be, a way for you to choose what mood you want to be in. You need a hypnotic power song.

Have you ever had a tune run through your head and couldn't get it out? The application is simple. Just pick a song (just one is best to begin with) that makes the emotions you want and deliberately play it in your mind when you want.

Make it loud, bright, whatever it takes to get you feeling exactly how you want. Rehearse it with your eyes closed. Play with it intensely until every time you hear that song in your head you feel exactly how you want to.

You will surprise yourself how quickly you can decide not only to be happy, but what kind of happiness you want!

Have a personal trance song!

Craig Rovinsky

HypnoJournal

LOVE TRANCES

What is Hypnotic Trance?

Let me take you through a hypnotism show from a hypnotist's point of view. Then we'll examine these principles in the rest of the book, revealing the secrets, and showing you how to do what I do on stage in the normal course of your daily life.

It's a high school lock-in party for graduation and the show is in the gym at 3 a.m. I'm dressed so I look great, and I feel fantastic inside. I'm psyched to have fun and I am feeling very playful.

I'm introduced and walk into the applause of about 500 people. As I walk in, I am scanning the audience for people who seem to be feeling what I am. I try to remember as many as I can. Most of the audience is already in a trance! "In just a few moments, we are going to have some of you up here on stage to be hypnotized, mesmerized, and circum . . . stances permitting, having a good time," I begin. Even with the crowd already halfway in trance, I spend some time talking about hypnotism, telling stories, and as I talk, I feel the trust and bond between myself and the audience increase. They know I am an expert and feel safe to have a magical, new experience. It is time to begin.

I have everyone put his or her hands together, prayer-fashion, fingers interlaced and closed over each hand. I have them raise the index fingertips, hold them and inch or

Craig Rovinsky

so apart, focus on the tips and imagine little magnets pulling them together.

This works easily on almost everyone. Having this experience sets a nice brain state for what comes next.

I now choose whom I wish for the stage from those who are having the most fun. They sit in a line, twenty people who want to expand their idea of what they thought was possible. I can see from their faces that most already have a characteristic look.

> This "trance look" expression consists of complete relaxation of facial muscles.

I will do a formal induction because it is expected of me, though I know it isn't necessary. In my talk, I have paced their reality and made them feel safe. In my fingertips test I have made them bypass their conscious mind to the point where their imagination became their reality. There really isn't a magnet in their fingertips, but they are still attracted to each other! During the induction I take their minds to new realities and begin the experiments.

In the next 45 minutes reality shifts as they experience the belief that their shoes are on the wrong feet, music is coming from their shoes, and their feet are where their ears are and they must put their shoes on.

LOVE TRANCES

They eat ice cream in a speed-eating contest, forget and remember the wrong names, and speak and interpret Martian. They are four years old, then 100 years old. They race camels and dance in championships, winning cars. A guy falls in love with a microphone stand. Their belly buttons vanish, butts appear and disappear, and we only met twenty minutes ago!

Then come the post-hypnotic suggestions. After removing them from trance I send them back to their chairs (except for one person that I left stuck to his chair). Key words trigger installed behaviors and more action ensues. I say "red," and one guy begins to start yelling warnings about the creature from the black lagoon coming. "Yellow!" triggers another to a rousing rendition of "God Bless America," and "blue" causes someone to loudly begin hawking miniature kangaroos. All this is going on simultaneously while the one on stage is trying to get out of his chair. Finally, it's time to release everyone.

I yell "green" and everyone who was in the show jumps up and yells, "Wow, I could have had a V-8!" The trance vanishes, they stand amazed, and the crowd goes wild. Hypnotism rocks.

This is done with total strangers; takes less than an hour and they know generally what I am going to do in advance. It's going to be a lot easier for you.

Craig Rovinsky

My Secret Confession

I have a confession. A secret life. Something I enjoy doing that no one knows about. Every so often, sometimes at home, sometimes in the car, I like to put music on. I like it a little loud. I get into it. I really, really get into it. When I am at home, I dance.

Have you ever got into music so much you just forgot where you were and danced? The beat starts to get you and your mind and body are totally into the emotion and you are rockin'! The whole universe is you and your music. You are the world's greatest dancer!

You've had this experience too? You don't tell anyone. It's just your secret way to have fun from time to time. Remember that stage show? One of the things each of my subjects did was to become the world's greatest dancer. The experience they have on stage is the same experience you and I have when we are alone at home, dancing to our favorite song on the radio.

> When you are dancing, totally absorbed and oblivious to the world you are having the exact same internal experience as the hypnotized person on stage.

LOVE TRANCES

The reaction of a hypnotized "dance contest winner" who has been told he's won a car is identical to someone who is actually winning a car on "The Price is Right." The internal experience is the same. It is not dependent on objective reality, but on what a person believes to be reality. In trance states, the conscious mind checks out and the unconscious mind, which believes everything it is told, takes control of the person.

My boyfriend and I broke up. He wanted to get married, and I didn't want him to.
Rita Rudner

What is Trance?

Trance is the state of total absorption in a narrow field of focus to the extent that external reality ceases to exist.

Total absorption + narrow focus = Trance

The state of total absorption, once achieved, can be maintained, while the focus is changed, thus changing the perceived reality.

The act of changing the focus will automatically link the result to you.

Craig Rovinsky

You don't have to be the source of the trance, just the source of the change of focus.

It is often associated with a good imagination, but it is really the intensity of absorption into a thought or thing that produces a trance state.

Things that are imagined while in trance are more real in your mind than what is right in front of you. How many times have you taken a walk or drive and not remembered anything you saw? You will have in your mind whatever you were thinking about but what you physically saw in front of you didn't register.

It is a matter of recognizing existing trance, or creating a trance. Once he is in this super-impressionable brain state, you amplify what you choose in his heart and mind. These feelings will automatically link to you as the source.

There are many types of trance states. If you are a woman who has ever seen a man watch sports, you have seen one of the most obvious forms of daily trance men experience. They yell at the TV. Just who does he think he's yelling at and what does he think will happen if they hear him? That's a trance. There sure isn't much thinking going on in his brain at moments like these.

Next time you feel spaced-out, check your vision. You will notice that there is a "tunnel"

LOVE TRANCES

effect. Your peripheral vision will be limited. This effect is said to be a sign of hypnotic trance, yet if you consciously check throughout your day, you will frequently find yourself experiencing it. Does that mean you spend most of your day in a trance?

Yes. This is the most important realization you will ever make in your life, especially regarding your love life.

> People are trance machines, going from one hypnotic state to another with a few moments of awareness between.

"Waking" trance is no different from a stage trance. Remember how I mentioned that most people in my audience are usually already in trance? The issue isn't whether they are already hypnotized, but what trance they are currently experiencing and how deeply they are experiencing it.

Everyone who has had that experience of dancing alone to music has been in a waking trance. It is a useful property of human beings that stage hypnotists have used for centuries in order to entertain. Furthermore, there are many other trances that do not physically manifest themselves but are just as powerful inside a person's mind.

Many people have the belief they cannot be hypnotized. This comes from some

17

Craig Rovinsky

university studies of "hypnotic susceptibility." For the study they used the same recorded induction. They ignored the idea that everyone might trance differently.

Think of it like music. You got a white guy, short hair, driving a pickup and blasting country western. Or you might have rap coming from the car of a dark chocolate angel. Everyone trances deeply and they do so differently from anyone else.

> Once you know what to look for, you can find the trances that exist in another and make wonderful things happen in both of your lives.

By accessing the trance states in someone's mind that trigger deep soul-to-soul connection, then linking them to you, you can mine his heart and create love for both of you.

The choice is yours. You can settle for a one-in-five chance at love, or you can take control of your love life. You can screen candidates by asking key questions that get at his core trances. Then you can decide whether to proceed with one man or move on to another, more suitable person. And, when you do find that special man, you will be able to create unbreakable bonds of love between you.

LOVE TRANCES

*I don't believe in luck. We make our own good
fortune.*
Joyce Brothers

Is it manipulation? Is it unscrupulous? It depends on how you decide to use these techniques. If someone tries to get me to do something that will ultimately make me a happier person, that's being thoughtful. If they are trying to get me to do something I don't want to do, that's manipulation.

To be perfectly blunt, the techniques I will teach you could be used in a manipulative way. Waking trance is a powerful tool with potential for abuse, just as fire or a car could be put to good or bad uses. You are 100% responsible for your actions. My hope is that everyone reading Love Trances will use its powerful techniques to create the deep, lasting love they deserve.

If you abuse trance, you will rapidly regret it. If you create a deep bond before you carefully screen a potential mate you could bond yourself to a Frankenstein. What I will teach you in Love Trances works very powerfully, but be careful what you wish for...

*I turned down a date once because I was
looking for someone higher up on the food
chain.*
Judy Tenuta

Craig Rovinsky

Are You in a Trance Now?

If you ever want to know how deep of a trance you are in, try this. Sit quietly and just relax your peripheral vision. Notice things at the edges of your vision.

Now, let go of that for a bit. Next, focus on making your hearing a little more sensitive. Listen for the tiny things you would normally ignore.

Next, do both at the same time, relaxing both your peripheral vision and hearing at the same time. Just allow those senses to experience everything by relaxing into it.

It's different from your normal experience, isn't it? It won't take long before the hearing gets filtered again, the peripheral vision tunnels, and you are back to living your life deep inside your head, in a trance. It probably won't take more than a minute. Don't worry. You are normal. We all do it, but men's trances occur more often and are deeper than women's. Starting to sound a little easier?

Bad News and Good News

First the bad news: it is a little harder for most men to make emotional connections than it is for most women. I'm sure you've already noticed that. The good news for you is that men go into trance easier and deeper. Once you know how to use waking trance, it

LOVE TRANCES

will be easier to connect with their hearts than you ever believed possible.

Men are practically helpless against the techniques you will learn. Stage hypnotists will tell you that frequently the best hypnotism shows are composed of mostly male subjects (though everyone really watches the women closest). It's because men go deeper into their personal trances and get there faster. It is no different in daily life.

A Day In the Life of an Empty Mind

Sometimes you'll go inside a man's mind and it will seem there is nothing there. It may be just an odd day, or there may really be nothing there. Remember that I said that about one in five guys are not an option when it comes to a relationship?

A palm reading client told me she read a magazine survey. It indicated that one out of five men wanted a different woman every night. (This ratio was higher in bars, lower with personal friend introductions).

My experience with thousands of women in palm readings confirms this. Some men, for whatever reasons, just have limited connection and compassion abilities. Wouldn't it be nice to find this out in the first fifteen minutes after meeting him, instead of three months later?

Craig Rovinsky

There will be days when it seems the number is larger than one in five. Some days it is. Once you realize that the fact that your not meeting quality men isn't your fault, you've taken a giant step toward becoming your own romance heroine.

You are going to start by using existing trances that already have strong impact in his mind. When you get more advanced, you will begin creating entirely new trance states in him that his mind assigns exclusively to you.

So, how do you start any journey? With the first step. When you first meet a potential partner, what do you say? When do you say it? How do you obtain trance states without him noticing? That's the subject of our next chapter, Conversation 101. Let's talk . . .

LOVE TRANCES

What You Should Know From This Chapter

There is little difference between stage hypnotism and covert or conversational hypnotism.

People spend most of their lives in trance.

Men go into trance deeper and faster than women.

Trance is the state of total absorption in a narrow field of focus to the extent that external reality ceases to exist.

Total absorption + Narrow Focus = Trance

Hypnotic Homework

Earlier in this chapter we talked about relaxing your peripheral vision and hearing to experience how deep a trance you are usually in. Take a few minutes now and do the exercise. Give yourself a new experience today.

Craig Rovinsky

HypnoJournal

LOVE TRANCES

Basic Conversational Hypnosis 101

So what do you say and when do you say it? The first thing to increase your conversational confidence is knowing what you are going to say.

> Having an outline that can take you through fifteen minutes of strong conversation with someone you just met is invaluable.

By not worrying about what you are going to say you can pay attention to their responses and decide if this person deserves your further attention. We will discuss the basic outline to get you started fast, and then go into more detail throughout the book as your understanding grows. The first part will be techniques. In the second part we will look at what you can do with your new powers.

How to Hypnotize Someone With Just a Look

Before you even speak there is something you must learn. You may have heard of a

Craig Rovinsky

special "look" a hypnotist can give someone so they begin to go into a trance. It's true. Silent hypnosis is gentle, soft, and easy. When I meet my volunteers on stage I take a few seconds and do this with each person as I walk from chair to chair meeting them and shaking their hand. It makes people feel they like and trust you, in just seconds. There are two parts to the look.

The first part of the look is your body language. Imagine you are trying to physically expose your heart to the person you are speaking with. If they are angled away, you still face them with this open posture.

> By thinking in your mind that you are trying to physically expose your heart it gives you the subconscious body language that triggers trust from him.

Think to yourself you are trying to send warmth to him from your heart. If you have another emotion you want to use, that's O.K. too, but when you aren't sure, warmth is a good one. Not overeager, but gentle warmth and curiosity are the feelings you want to project.

The second part of the look, the eyes, magnifies this effect. Have you ever wanted hypnotic eyes? Pick one of his eyes. Start

LOVE TRANCES

with the eye furthest from you because the closest eye might be too intense right away. You want to look into his eye and notice what color it is, what variations are in it. Actually think to yourself what color his eyes are.

This curiosity will give you just the right amount of gentle but strong eye contact. Obviously, every so often you need to break off intimate eye contact and 'scan back' to a more normal eye contact. Still, start with this type of eye contact and come back to it frequently.

So you are introduced, you do your hypnotic look, shake his hand and repeat his name.

If you've never learned to do a good handshake, here's how. Take his hand in yours, palm to palm. Your fingers should curl around the back of his hand at least partially, depending on the relative size of your hands. Apply gentle pressure to the bones on the back of his hand that you can reach. Pump twice and release.

Unless you have a specific reason, do this sequence every time. **Repeat his name so you don't forget it** (a real trance-breaker). The handshake will give you a huge amount of "feel" on him, especially if you are strongly

27

Craig Rovinsky

in the open heart body position. It's hard to describe. Experiment with it a few times. Once you get the hang of it, you will shake hands every time you meet someone new. A handshake is actually used by professional hypnotists as a type of induction. Brain in neutral, mind waiting for input . . . that's a trance state, and precisely the state you get for a moment with a handshake.

> That moment when he is shaking your hand, looking in your eyes and waiting for your name, his brain is in a trance.

That is the moment you really beam your warmth as you give your name. Relax back to normal open warmth and continue the conversation. You will only need seconds to weed out some, or find that others may be worth more time. That special moment is a knack, but not hard to achieve. As you will gain access to so many trances during handshake moments in your life, it's a good feel to learn to recognize.

Make love in the microwave. Think how much time you'll save.
Carly Simon

LOVE TRANCES

How to Talk to a Total Stranger

Assuming you got at least a reasonable feel from the handshake it's time to talk. I will give you a basic outline, then talk about how the application differs, depending on whether or not you develop an interest in him. These are the trance topics.

1] Location/occasion
2] Occupation
3] Where did you grow up?

Quite simple, isn't it? For some reason otherwise confident people find themselves in situations where they don't know what to say. It is because they haven't internalized any topics, such as these.

Memorize them, all three of them. At any moment you should be able to pull these topics out without searching. Let's see what you can do with these simple trance topics.

Trance Topic One: Location/Occasion

This is just the reason why you are both there, perhaps a play, a concert or party. It is the perfect opener to a conversation, just comment on something you are both experiencing, *external* to either of you.

"What do you think of the centerpiece?" may sound simple, but it does something important, other than start the conversation.

Craig Rovinsky

Before you started to talk to him, who knows where his mind was?

You've interrupted whatever direction his mind was going with the handshake, and bought him to a "brain neutral" state. Now, by commenting on something external to either of you his thoughts are starting to follow your direction. You're not doing bad, considering this is a total stranger you met less than thirty seconds ago!

It is important to note that it is an open-ended question, a question requiring an explanation, rather than a simple yes/no. The explanation keeps his mind open and going the direction you want. Yes/no questions have the opposite effect, closing down the mind most of the time.

> When you comment on something external make it a sound, if you can. The act of changing awareness from primarily visual to auditory creates a trance. Try it now. Listen for sounds you would normally tune out. As you listen closely notice how your awareness changes.

Now you listen. If you talk too much here, you will ruin it. You must give them a chance to open up. Your eye contact and body language is often all it takes to get

LOVE TRANCES

someone talking. Whatever they respond with, agree.

The only exception is if their answer isn't one you are comfortable agreeing with. In that case, they may be screening themselves out already.

It depends on the emotional tone of the answer. If you aren't sure, just continue the conversation. If it hasn't started its own life yet (many conversations need a bit more to start) then go immediately into . . .

Trance Topic Two: Occupation

Once he has briefly talked about what he does, think three things: past, present, and future. Specifically, you ask him...

Past: How did you start in this?
Present: What are your challenges?
Future: What does the future look like?

Use these questions, or others that address past, present, and future with open-ended questions. What a man does, or plans to do for a living, is core to him. Men feel they are judged by their occupations in society so questions that go to this emotional core will affect him deeply. (Have you ever run into a man who exaggerated his wealth or possessions to try to impress you)? You will be able to touch him emotionally like no one else has.

Craig Rovinsky

Listen very closely when he talks of his present challenges. That will tell you where he is at emotionally and how he approaches problems in life. He will also give you solid gold trance words.

The last question, the future question, will give you a sense of his belief in his own possibilities. Many, many men will rule themselves out when you discover their core. So you wasted fifteen minutes on them. Be glad it wasn't six weeks. Even with this simplified conversation structure you will be accessing deep trance states.

This last part, past-present-future, of the occupation question can turn a fifteen-minute conversation into hours. Finding a core business interest and asking him, "How did you ever get started in...?" is one of the easiest ways to get him to open up. It is so strong it can be difficult to get away from him once he starts telling you, so use it only on men you want to be around a while.

A Palm Reader's Secret

It is no surprise that most women have love on their mind when they go to a palm reader. What isn't so well known is most men have some idea (good or screwy) to make money. Asking if he ever had an idea for a business of his own can be very productive. (Ask him about it, but whatever you do, don't loan him money to do it!)

LOVE TRANCES

What do you do if he doesn't like his job? If that is the case there are two things to remember. First, spend extra time on the future and his career dreams. Trust me, he has thought about it.

Second, you are looking for a certain positive attitude of how he handles challenges. It isn't as important that he doesn't like his current job. It is more important to see how he meets his challenges.

Trance Topic Three: Where Did You Grow Up?

If things are winding down and you don't want anything to do with him, this is a good exit point. On the other hand, if you want to go for a deeper connection from this first conversation here is where you do it.

"Where did you grow up?", while apparently innocent, has another purpose. Asking someone where they grew up requires them to access memories.

In the introduction you put his brain in neutral, location/occasion allowed you to begin to control the direction of his thoughts. Now you are sending him inside. By asking him where he grew up, you are on safe ground. With questions about where he grew up you will control which memories he accesses. If he had a miserable, abusive childhood, you don't trigger those memories.

33

Craig Rovinsky

So now you are talking to him about where he grew up. What did he play at most? Who were his friends? If he seems to be guarded or tense, it is a sign there may be more there. He may be reliving nasty childhood experiences. This is a potential danger sign. This person may be very negative or angry at something.

If, on the other hand, he seems to be worth further investigation, here is where you start to go to work. For you to have an impact he has to have strong, positive, emotional experiences when he is with you, and he has to associate them to you. Since he is already in a deep internal stage, reliving childhood memories in his mind, other strong, positive memories can now be accessed.

> When he vividly relives a memory, he relives the emotions that came with that memory. He will associate these emotions with the one who triggered the memories and, by listening, allowed him to relive the memories...you.

You can't go straight for this deep trance immediately after the handshake. You must have a brain state that is conducive to accessing those states, complete with the emotions that went with them. If you try for

LOVE TRANCES

this too early, he will be uncomfortable, or at minimum, will be unable to emotionally open up to you.

His existing trance state determines what his reaction will be when you go for the emotions.

You now ask him what his happiest memories in childhood were and just be willing to listen and play in this topic.

He who hesitates is a damn fool.
Mae West

I must address a sensitive issue here. It is so important I will repeat it several times throughout the book. Too much talk here is deadly. Remember what you are trying to accomplish. If you are talking nonstop you will never have the chance to touch him emotionally. I understand that sometime you have so much to share you just can't help it, but consider this. When you dominate the conversation you drive him away. When you listen, you bring him closer. More active listening will reveal his personal trances to you. This will allow you into his heart, when other women have talked his heart shut, wondering why he doesn't open up.

Craig Rovinsky

The Bounce

To illustrate the power of listening let me tell you a story. I knew a used-car salesman, Jeffro, who loved to partner with another salesman and play what they called "bounce."

Two salesmen would stand either side of a customer. One would cross his arms and not make eye contact while the other adopted the heart-body language and eye contact, showing he was listening. The customer would give his full attention to the one who seemed to be listening.

At a given signal the salesmen would shift roles, changing their listening body language so that the one previously listening would cross his arms and break eye contact and the other would assume the listening characteristics. The customer's attention would "bounce" from one person to another without being aware of it.

There was no break in the conversation, just an unconscious shift. The salesmen would bounce the customer's attention back and forth, playing a strange, psychic game of catch. I always thought that Jeffro really needed a better hobby. Still, it illustrates my point. Remember that this was all done with silent listening signals!

Listening is really that powerful. If you master the art of listening, you will be able to capture men's hearts in ways other women

LOVE TRANCES

can only dream of. Fortunately, it is very simple to be a good listener.

During a conversation, remember to wait a full two to three seconds after he finishes talking before replying. Give him a chance to finish his thoughts. The more you let him talk, the easier it will be for you to form a connection with him later if you decide you would like to keep him.

The Listening Breath

A technique exists to help you listen. It is called the listening breath. Simply put, when you are listening breath normally on the inhale. When you exhale, do it slowly and relaxed. Lengthen your exhale and you will discover your brain chatter slows down significantly. This allows you to focus more effectively and easily experience the incredible charisma of being a good listener.

Craig Rovinsky

What You Should Know From This Chapter

The open-heart/handshake combination is a gentle trance induction.

Conversation outline:

Location/occasion

Occupation Past/Present/Future

Where did you grow up?

Most men have some idea for a business that is a core trance for them.

Learn and use the listening breath.

Hypnotic Homework

Memorize the basic conversation outline until comfortable with it. You can practice with anyone. It doesn't have to be a potential mate.

LOVE TRANCES

HypnoJournal

Craig Rovinsky

LOVE TRANCES

Conversation 102 Advanced Techniques

IMPORTANT RULE OF CONVERSATIONAL HYPNOSIS: MEN HAVE <u>VERY</u> FRAGILE EGOS WHEN IT COMES TO CONTROL ISSUES. NEVER TELL HIM YOU KNOW CONVERSATIONAL HYPNOSIS.

So, you've talked to him a while and have decided you want to hypnotize him to be your favorite love toy. You will be able to do that but for now let's start with the basics.

I don't want to beat a deadbeat dad (or is that a dead horse?) but I must emphasize it is very important to have a deep understanding that there is no difference between what you see on stage and the deep daydreams and fantasies you experience yourself.

The internal process is the same . . . an internal focus (or spaced-out, total absorption in nothingness), very few different thoughts occurring, but those that are occurring are repeated in various forms. Those that are repeated can become so vivid that you forget they are fantasies (stage hypnotism making more sense now?)

Try it now. Take a deep breath, exhale, relax, and close your eyes (after reading the instructions). Choose a specific memory for

41

Craig Rovinsky

you that was fantastic in some way. Stop now and think of a really good one . . . then make it brighter, louder, bigger. Feel the emotions and sensations of your memory. Repeat it over and over in your mind <u>until you are totally absorbed in the memory</u>. Do whatever it takes to have as much of the experience as you can. Just close your eyes and enjoy that memory as real as you can now . . . stop now and give yourself a special treat. Make yourself happy for no reason at all!

Be honest, didn't parts of that memory get very real in a very short time? Heck, I did the exercise after I wrote it and I can't show you my relaxed smile, but believe me, it's there.

As a matter of fact, there's a good chance we had a similar internal emotion, you and I felt the same deep feeling. When you have the same nice, internal experience as someone else it makes you feel a warm connection, even if you just met on a page of paper.

It isn't hard to do.

Some of us are becoming the man we wanted to marry.
Gloria Steinem

I remember a 20'ish woman who came in for a palm reading. She was very upset and frantically said she needed a reading

LOVE TRANCES

immediately. She didn't have a particular question; she was just feeling scattered and panicky.

I started by a moment of silence, supposedly to let me focus but really to get her to stop hyperventilating. I did a yoga breath that calmed me (basically a long, slow exhale), and could feel her relaxing as I relaxed.

I commented on something on her hand. She had a mark on her hand that made me feel she wanted to be a ballerina when a little girl. It is a common little girl's dream, as you might think.

The real purpose was not to be "psychic", but to get her reliving a positive childhood experience. I didn't even use advanced techniques to get her to relive it. I just listened.

The reading was about 2 minutes of palm reading, and 28 of listening to her and how beautiful she felt as a little girl ballerina. I just listened and cared. I have names for various types of hands. I now call her hand a "ballerina hand." I told her at the time that was her hand, the ballerina hand, and she would always take these beautiful feelings with her. She left feeling like the ballerina that was always in her heart.

Men are my hobby; if I ever got married I'd have to give it up.
Mae West

Craig Rovinsky

Million-Dollar Inductions for Free

Many examples of conversational hypnosis can be found in national TV commercials. If you watch closely, there are two hypnotic techniques that are commonly used.

The first is creating brain neutral, and then imprinting the message. A commercial that is trying this will start a story that you find interesting, but you can't figure out where it is going. You watch, often wondering what the hell they are advertising. It is that blatant. Still, when the time comes for the message, your brain is wide open, searching for meaning, and the message goes in.

> Unsatisfied curiosity creates a powerful trance state.

I remember seeing a foreign commercial, Swedish, I think. It had a couple in the bedroom and they were starting to get really friendly. The enthusiasm kept building until they were really into it. It was plants falling over, books crashing from the shelves, bed being torn apart, people taking kids off the street kind of sex. Suddenly things got real quiet. After a few seconds of deep relaxed

LOVE TRANCES

breathing came the message. It was an ad for a newspaper.

The second is emotional trance transference. The commercial might show hot music, sexy dancers and hard bodies. It's a party! This goes on for twenty to twenty-five seconds of a thirty-second commercial, trying to create an excited state in you. At the very end of the commercial the product pops in and your emotions transfer to the product. Dr. Pepper ™ is great for this type of ad. They are very good at this induction.

Advertisers have measured responses and tracked brain waves to discover this. There are many other techniques but these two basic, obvious hypnotic inductions sell millions of dollars of product each year. They are also quite good for transferring emotions from one person to another. Think about how you might use these inductions in your daily life.

I told my wife the truth. I told her I was seeing a psychiatrist. Then she told me the truth: that she was seeing a psychiatrist, two plumbers and a bartender.
Rodney Dangerfield

Silent Hypnosis

Now that you are getting a feel for what we are doing practice the open-heart body position with notice-the-color eye contact,

Craig Rovinsky

from the previous chapter. Keep this playful and fun so you'll smile. With this look alone you can create brain neutral. Many people will trance out even stronger, going deep inside to that place where they store feelings of trust, and assign those feelings to you.

The degree to which this happens depends on you getting the right emotional tone projected from your heart, amplified gently through your eyes. Imagine a connection between the two of you, a beam of energy (or white or pink light, or whatever works for you) connecting the two of you with your hearts and eyes connecting. You'll know you have it when you go to shift your gaze and your eyes seems a little "sticky," stuck slightly to contact with his eyes.

The other factor in this equation is the other person. As mentioned earlier, some guys just don't have anything inside or what is in there is twisted and demented. You'll feel that, too. It isn't necessary to say a word to create a nice, gentle, strong trance with the hypnotic look.

I take care of myself, because I learned early on that I am the only person in life who's responsible for me.
Halle Berry

With a little practice, you can now literally hypnotize men with just a glance. Some women do this naturally, not knowing why

LOVE TRANCES

they are so hypnotic to men. Next time you see someone like this, watch her heart and eyes. You'll see her doing something similar, probably without being aware of it.

So now you have some version of brain neutral or light trance. The degree you have their focus on you, entranced, will decide the impact of what follows. Without brain neutral, what follows are just conversation topics. With brain neutral these are hypnotic inductions.

The trance state he is in will determine his response. Brain state guides reaction in all situations.

Advanced Hypnotic Conversation

As you now have a better understanding of trance, lets play a bit with the conversation outline.

It's time for location/occasion. Remember, by commenting on something external to either of you his attention will be external and whatever was going on inside his mind before you arrived ceases to be important or even exist. Already at this early stage you could be handed gold. Here is an example.

One of my palm reading clients, Tina, came to me with a problem. Tina was a small

Craig Rovinsky

girl, thirty-one years old, about 5' 2" and thin, with shoulder-length brown hair. It was obvious from spending just a few minutes reading her palm that she had it together emotionally, but still had something very important on her mind. She hadn't had sex in twelve years.

It wasn't from lack of opportunity, but choice. She was very independent and insisted on a certain level of quality, but she could never tell if a man was sincere. She certainly wasn't waiting for marriage; in fact she wanted an adventure for herself.

She didn't need a knight in shining armor, but a knight in rusty armor was just too much. Though most of the men took themselves out of it by being obvious she felt there had to be someone out there who was more than a male gland.

I taught her the basic handshake/three step conversation. A few months later I saw her and we had coffee. She was glowing.

"I learned what you taught me," she began. "Frankly, I didn't believe you when you told me I could hypnotize men without their knowledge. This is so easy I am almost embarrassed I wasted those years. What I am looking for, and what I am not looking for often is obvious when I comment on location/occasion. It seems when a man is externally oriented he lets his guard down. Whatever line he was going to throw at me is put on hold while his mind processes the

LOVE TRANCES

external reality necessary to answer my question. With my heart open, I can feel what he is like as a person in that moment. I can't tell specifics, but when he goes back into 'conversation' mode he reveals much."

<u>"If the feeling when he is externally oriented match the feeling when he is internally oriented it is a good sign</u>. A mismatch indicates someone who isn't being sincere from the beginning, someone who is putting up a front. Using this knowledge, I know who I want to talk to further. I haven't been disappointed." Sincerity is very important to her.

I had to ask. "It's been twelve years . . . well . . .?"

Tina replied, "I've always had control over my public life. I now have control in my private life. I have options and no longer have to consider if I should just give up and settle for what comes along."

"So . . .?", I asked.

Tina just smiled. Tina always had a nice smile. It just seems happier these days.

I must admit I never considered that occasion/location could be applied that way. I've always used the concept to just start directing the attention of those on stage and taught others to do the same in regular conversation.

Tina took that simple first step and made it much better. She looked for the difference between the "emotional feel" when he was

Craig Rovinsky

externally oriented, as compared to the feel when he was internally oriented. When there was little or no difference she felt this was a sign he was being honest. Big differences indicated he was putting up a front to try to impress her. Honesty is a very good start for a relationship.

The second question, "Occupation", is pretty well dealt with using the concept of past-present-future, so let's go to the next question.

As the third question, "where did you grow up," can already have powerful impact let me digress now and talk about the process of love. It's important to understand what you are doing as it relates to falling in love.

> For most people falling in love happens when the other person is not present.

You might have a good time with someone and as time goes you think they were OK, but nothing great. Another person may touch you deeply for a few moments, at a few separate times, then go back to normal conversation.

Still, as the next few days pass, you find yourself thinking about them, reliving those few moments of emotional intimacy over and

LOVE TRANCES

over. Your mind, like mine, fills in the blanks. It is that process you will be using.

Since few women can touch a man emotionally at all, much less in a few minutes, he will be thinking of you like he has never thought of anyone else. To repeat, be careful what you ask for. He will fall in love with you when you are not around.

One other point concerns your own heart. It is very easy to hypnotize yourself that you love someone. Your ability to form an emotional connection is seldom an issue. What is important is now you have choices. Desperation is deadly to love relationships. If you are coming from a point of desperation, predatory men will still sniff you out.

Later we will talk about some hypnosis you can do for yourself, what I call "useful hallucinations." For now, just realize that with waking hypnosis your love life can go from starvation, having to accept what you get, to a gourmet banquet. You will no longer ask yourself "does he like me?", but rather, "is he good enough for me?" You need to start being picky, not every man is good enough for you.

There will be some men you run into that do have a few good things going for them. Every relationship doesn't have to end in marriage. Sometimes it is good to have practice relationships. Learn what you can at that time of your life. Let things unfold without worrying if this is "the one", or

51

Craig Rovinsky

wondering if your family will approve. Every so often it is good for you to lightly play.

> "Is he good enough for me?" is a very useful attitude for most women.

Often, when you just listen people will give you their personal trance words. Let me give you an unexpected example.

A while back my wife and I took my mother to Casper, Wyoming to visit family. Later, my mother and I were talking about it on the phone. The subject of trance words came up and we had this conversation.

"Mom, when I remember you in Casper I remember seeing you sitting out on the front porch in the wooden rocking chair. You were all bundled up against the desert winter and were wearing that wool hat you got in the airport on the way out. You were smoking a cigarette and looked so happy. What was that like?"

"Peaceful. Very peaceful."

I repeated, "Peaceful."

Mom said, ". . . yeah . . ." You could actually hear her relax over the phone. Though I had told her what I was doing beforehand, she didn't mind at all. She felt peaceful. Let's look at how I did that.

LOVE TRANCES

The Anatomy of a Telephone Induction

The conversation began normally with standard topics. Then something had made us laugh really hard. At that point, right after the laughter, the brain is in a good mood and in neutral. I directed her thoughts by setting the scene in Casper and went deep on the description to bring it to life. Naming something makes it real as they must represent it in their mind. Next, describing it brings it alive. By the time I got to the end of the description she was reliving the experience and thus relived the emotion.

While most people will give you several personal trance words, my Mom gave just one. Do you think I am going to do all I can to try make my Mom feel peaceful from now on? Do you think it will be hard to get her to tell me what makes her feel that way? Do you think her life will be much happier as a result? Is there anyone in your life you could make happier by listening closely?

Craig Rovinsky

What You Should Know From This Chapter

Never let a man know you can hypnotize him.

The trance he is in will determine his responses.

Falling in love happens when the other person isn't around.

Be careful not to hypnotize yourself you are in love.

"Is he good enough for me?" is a great attitude for most women.

Personal trance words are the easiest key to his heart.

Hypnotic Homework

Listen for personal trance words through the day. Just give yourself a chance to see how easy it is once you know what you are looking for.

LOVE TRANCES

HypnoJournal

Craig Rovinsky

LOVE TRANCES

Love Trances From His Childhood

Here is how you get trance words from "where did you grow up?" Assuming it isn't obvious from his reaction that childhood was horrible, he'll tell you where he grew up. It is an innocent question, but by doing the mental process to answer it, his mind is headed toward his having a deep experience he will enjoy, while revealing his trance words to you.

After he responds, he will continue to talk about where he grew up. If he doesn't, just ask him to tell you about it. So, what was it like growing up in Uzbekistan?

You now listen carefully. Frequently you will get trance words without doing anything else.

> How do you know when you have a trance word? It is a word that is usually an emotion that they lean on or emphasize.

For my mother it was peaceful. You can tell because they will put more emphasis on the words. If they lean heavily on a word which isn't an obvious emotion just look a little deeper for the emotion behind the word.

57

Craig Rovinsky

One of my clients told me she was talking to a guy and the word he leaned on was Ford. For most that doesn't trigger an emotion but he absolutely loved his Ford cars. If someone used that word with him, they would receive the emotions he experiences with the word Ford transferred to the object of the sentence. Huh?

In other words, if you were to say to him (when he is brain neutral or trance), "You are the Ford in my life," you would be very pleased with the response. (Of course, you have him in a trance state before you ask him this to magnify the effect, but you already know that!)

THE SINGLE MOST POWERFUL AREA TO CREATE RAPID EMOTIONAL CONNECTIONS IS POSITIVE CHILDHOOD EXPERIENCES.

Childhood photo albums are great sources of memories. Keep your ears open for positive childhood nicknames and music he liked when going through puberty, also.

Advertisers love to go for age regression. They know how sending someone into a childlike state will make them very happy and very open to suggestion. One commercial for cars shows a child. The "spokes child", a child in an adult business

LOVE TRANCES

suit, just looks into the camera and goes, "Zoom, zoom, zoom." Then the car name is given.

Always be aware when listening to someone's childhood memories. They have great power. They contain screening information, trance words, time distortion, and age regression. There is a lot to work with in childhood memories.

Here are some verbal examples of "where did you grow up?"

> Y=you
> H=him

Y   So, where did you grow up?
Z   I grew up in the country near a small town in northern Alabama.

(After a second he doesn't expand so you, being you, decide to see if he is good enough for you . . .)

Y   What are your favorite memories from growing up there?
H   Well, being in the country there was a group of us who hung together. I remember being in control in that neighborhood. I had a lot of fun!

Let's see, he emphasized the word "control" and seemed to enjoy it. Maybe he is

Craig Rovinsky

for some woman but definitely not you! Next
. . .

Y So, where did you grow up?
H I grew up in Iowa City, Iowa. It was
great! My parents were grad students
and lived in married student housing.
There were swings, sand boxes, and
almost everyone there was a serious
student. The people were great and the
kids I grew up with were the kind of
friends you dream about.

Y Wow! It does sound great! Have any
memories you can share?
H Memories . . . let me think . . . I
remember this picnic. You see, in a
graduate community the population is
international and people are always
coming and going.

There was an Indonesian family that
had been there five years. Everyone
knew and loved them. Since they were
leaving, they threw a going-away
picnic. Many picnic tables were pulled
together in a common courtyard and
people came from everywhere with
food.

It was one of the best parties I was
ever at. At times it seemed no one

LOVE TRANCES

spoke the same language but there was this feeling that was wonderful.

Y What was that wonderful feeling like?

H Well, it was a warm, heart-to-heart feeling. I remember looking at a woman who I did not know. We spoke different languages, but on that sunny summer day we just looked at each other and felt good about being there.

Y Kind of like a summery feeling?

H Yea, kind of like that, a soft, summery feeling. Can I say that and still be a man?

Y Of course, there's nothing wrong with having a warm, heart-to-heart, soft, summery feeling. With me, it is a sign when I feel that way that it is some place I am supposed to be, and I just enjoy it.

You are well on your way to being a hypnotic seductress if you just understand these two, common scenarios. In the first his trance word was obviously control. Unless you are into that you know not to waste several months of your life there.

The next guy was far more interesting. The first word he leaned on was "great." She fed that back with, "It does sound great." She did the same with the word "wonderful" when he seemed to emphasize that. The use

61

Craig Rovinsky

of his own personal trance word opened him up. She goes on to use two conversational hypnosis techniques I will introduce now.

The Heart Mining Three-Deep

First the three-deep. She was looking to go past great and trying to find more words that will work as keys to his heart. When he went deeper, he gave her warmth, heart-to-heart, and soft.

> By asking up to three questions along the same emotional line you take a person very deep into trance.

Contrary to what some hypnotists say, depth of trance does matter...the deeper the absorption, the narrower the focus, the greater the result. His efforts to answer your questions require them to dig where the core trances that make up their identities live.

Be careful when you use the three-deep induction. Use it only on emotional areas you are relatively certain you want to open. This one induction can create deep attachment, so be careful. It seems I say that quite a bit, but I need to emphasize here this is not pie-in-the-sky fantasy. Waking hypnosis is very real power and irresponsibly used can backfire.

LOVE TRANCES

Repeat His Trance Words Back in Order

She used the second, simple technique of repeating his trance words back to him, in the order he gave them to her, warm, heart-to-heart, and soft.

Another example of this might be if a guy told you his ideal woman was independent, powerful, and still a little feminine. You would repeat right back, "So you are looking for a woman who is independent, powerful and still a little feminine?" That is no exaggeration, use as close to their exact words, especially their exact trance words, as you can.

When you ask them a question with their own trance words it makes them feel you understand them on a very deep level. You should be that blatant. Not only will they not care, they will love you for it. Obviously, you can get too carried away and sound like a parrot, but when you are using someone's personal trance words you can repeat much more than you would think.

It is basic, and repeating back their trance words in your own normal conversation is basic. Do it. Once you have trance words repeating them back in order days or weeks after you've learned them can have a massive impact. To him, you've just talked straight to his heart from out of the

63

Craig Rovinsky

blue. You can bet, as a guy, he doesn't remember much of a prior conversation.

Originally I was going to jokingly suggest that with men you get the same amnesia two hours after a conversation as you would in a woman in two months. It is true, though. With most men, you do not have to wait days or weeks to get them to forget they ever used those words around you. Repeating them back to him, in the order he gave them, in your very next sentence will work great on men. This is no exaggeration. Just use his trance words as soon as you can.

> Once you are on a thread of conversation that is giving you strong trance words keep on it. Continue to ask questions that concern emotional feelings or physical sensations. Mine it deep, deep, deep. Every time you take him deep into his heart and mind he will associate those pleasure feelings with you.

Transfer the Feelings to Yourself

She transferred those feelings to herself, just like in the soda commercial you get 25 seconds of sexy, passionate dance, then the product is shown and you associate the emotion with the product.

LOVE TRANCES

It does not have to be a logical connection. You only have to communicate you get the same feelings as he does, <u>and communicate it at the same exact moment he is experiencing those feelings</u>. The feelings will transfer and he will identify you as a source of those feelings. Sometimes you will get just a little transference; sometimes you will get instant love.

The variables here are your own skill, the physical and emotional state of the other person, and sometimes a touch of Irish luck. As you begin to notice these trances in peoples' everyday lives you will become skilled at using your intuition when you do your conversational inductions.

The combination of intuition and waking hypnosis is close to irresistible. You get there by practicing these concepts until they are second nature to you and become your normal style of conversation, always watching for core trances and trance words.

We will go over many more examples before we are done, but you have quite a bit to practice already. If you do nothing but what I have given you so far you will amaze yourself.

The next time you accidentally overhear a conversation, listen for trance words and watch people for trance states.

Craig Rovinsky

You will find they have been there all along, they are obvious, and you will find yourself growing into a hypnotic seductress with many new skills.

Dear United States Army:

My husband asked me to write a recommend that he support his family. He cannot read, so don't tell him. Just take him. He ain't no good to me. He ain't done nothing but raise hell and drink lemon essence since I married him eight years ago, and I got to feed seven kids of his. Maybe you can get him to carry a gun. He's good on squirrels and eating. Take him and welcome. I need the grub and his bed for the kids. Don't tell him this, but just take him.

Hand-delivered by an Arkansas man to his draft board—1943

LOVE TRANCES

What You Should Know From This Chapter

The single, most powerful area to create rapid emotional connections is positive childhood memories.

By asking up to three questions along the same emotional line you can create deep trance.

Hypnotic Homework

Help him access a pleasant childhood memory. Watch, listen, and think.

Craig Rovinsky

HypnoJournal

LOVE TRANCES

Hypnotic Keys to Unlock His Heart

In this chapter we will look at some of the "tools" available to you to induce a hypnotic trance in conversation. Though there may seem to be quite a few don't let it concern you. Just read through them. Some you will recognize once you are aware of them, often in commercials.

You don't have to memorize all these tools. Just try to understand what is happening as you are reading about them. Later you will develop favorites of your own.

Visual-Auditory-Kinesthetic

The first hypnotic key we will look at is the idea of visual-auditory-kinesthetic. Basically people access the world through a combination of these three senses.

In most people there is a preferred sense. In men the preferred sense is usually visual. In women it is usually kinesthetic. There are many exceptions to this.

How can you tell? The books tell you to listen for the type of words they lean on. Someone saying, "I feel . . ." is obviously in a kinesthetic mode. This doesn't always give you enough, though. An easier way to establish their primary filter is to listen to them speak.

69

Craig Rovinsky

<u>A fast talker, male or female, is very visual. A slow talker is very kinesthetic.</u>

<u>When a person is more talkative than normal for them, they are in a strong kinesthetic state.</u>

Most people talk somewhere in the middle, and have more balanced inputs. Auditory people do tend to be really obvious, showing it in their choice of words.

My own personal experience is those who are extremely auditory tend to be slightly eccentric and delightfully magical, but everyone is fun in their own way. When in doubt, assume the man is visually oriented.

Mirroring

The more a person subconsciously feels you are like them, the more they like and trust you. This is the second key. It is a primal circuit; things that are like me won't kill and eat me.

The things I have found work powerfully for mirroring includes breathing, rate of speech, head tilt, and posture.

Mirroring Breathing

Think about the last time you had a fantastically delicious physical experience. I'll bet you were breathing in a specific manner. Breathing patterns are directly tied

LOVE TRANCES

to the emotional centers. <u>If you mirror someone's breathing you will not only bond to them but will be able to feel what they are feeling</u>.

When a woman wants to mirror a man's breathing, it is simple. Just watch the chest. If for some reason you can't, watch the shoulders out of your peripheral vision. You don't need to stare, just check every so often.

After you do this a bit, you will get the hang of it and once you are mirroring his breathing you will find yourself automatically shifting your breathing rate when he shifts his.

Mirroring Rate of Speech

Closely related to breathing is mirroring his rate of speech. If you talk at the same rate as people do, they will like and trust you more. They can't help it. When you speak, you exhale. This has much the same effect as mirroring his breathing directly, but is far easier to do. Just try to talk at about the same rate as him, pausing in similar patterns. If you pick just one thing to mirror, this is the easiest.

Mirroring Head Tilt/Posture

Head tilt is easy. Match the tilt of their head with your own. You can be a bit bold about this. Just don't change the moment he changes. Move from one tilt to another gradually. If you identically parrot him, he

Craig Rovinsky

may notice. Just match his head tilt and motions in a general, slightly delayed way.

Body language is much the same. Just match it in a general way, body tilt and arm placement. You'll get to a place where you can feel the match pretty easily. That's as far as you need to go. If you match body language too exactly, it may start to feel odd to some people.

I want a man who's kind and understanding.
Is that too much to ask of a millionaire?
Zsa Zsa Gabor

Anchoring

Anchoring is another basic concept. It is Pavlov's dog, salivating at the ringing bell. Anchoring is most often seen in commercials. Do golden arches make you salivate (or want to hurl?)

The easiest way to anchor feelings is to express you have had the same feeling, while feeling that feeling inside you. When he is peaking, you anchor the feeling to an act (such as squeezing his hand), a look, or a phrase.

> An anchor is just something, such as a hand squeeze, that becomes associated with an emotion by happening at the same time as the emotion.

LOVE TRANCES

Immediately repeat the anchor. If it is a hand squeeze, do it again and beam that emotion to him. From now on, whenever you pause, have his attention and squeeze his hand you will trigger that emotion.

The degree this works to depends on the power of the initial anchor. Any anchor will work. It doesn't have to make sense.

If you are interested in a man who has an irrational passion for some sports team (those guys do exist) he will also have anchors to the colors that team wears. Do you think there is anything fun you could do with that knowledge?

Pacing and Leading

Pacing and leading are fundamental verbal skills. You acknowledge (pace) what he has just said, using trance words if possible. Then you lead deeper with a question on the same line.

Here is an example. Please note that the questions are seeking something kinesthetic, either an emotion or physical sensation. That is the key to drive them deeper.

Y. So you love the Packers? Why?

H. I grew up with my friends in the neighborhood and we always imagined we were the Packers in our street football games. I would get just as

Craig Rovinsky

excited about a touchdown as if I really were a player on the Packers.

Y. I know what you mean, I love getting that excited. Can you remember any great plays? (Guaranteed to drive him into another useful emotion).

H. Yes! (He is quite happy and very animated now. When's the last time someone made you feel that way? How did you feel about them?) There was a play I designed where everybody went out for a pass to the far corner of the end zone. That would leave me one-on-one with the guy who was supposed to pass-rush. He was always the same kid, big and strong but not too quick. I would just run around him and to the other corner of the end zone. Scoring a touchdown is such a rush!

Y. That seems like a great rush! What's it like?

H. You can feel the blood pumping, the adrenaline rushing through your veins, and there is something great just about winning.

We'll leave here, but now she has excitement, rush, and winning for power words. If she wanted to continue this line (and she should) she might say something like,

LOVE TRANCES

Y. I agree. I love winning! What's your biggest win ever?

Chances are it won't be in football and she has just opened up another direct path to his heart.

> Pace their statement, preferably with a trance word and lead with a question that goes to an emotion or physical sensation.

I wrote the story myself. It's about a girl who lost her reputation but never missed it.
Mae West

Quotes

Quotes add authority to things and allow you to say things that you normally wouldn't be able to. You can quote just about anything, TV, book, lecturer, etc. When you quote someone it is assumed they are an authority, but the biggest advantage of quotes, for our purposes is it allows you to bypass the conscious.

Quotes do this because when you are quoting someone their mind has to process the idea of someone else saying these words. The mind will make some representation of the other person in some manner.

Craig Rovinsky

While the mind is busy processing the quote within a small part of itself, it is not operating in conscious mode. It isn't a long trance time-wise, but it allows you to say things you wouldn't normally be able to get away with.

Y. I couldn't believe it. I was talking to my friend, Linda, and she told me . . .

His mind represents something for Linda so he can understand what you are going to say and you can now say anything, because after all, it is Linda that is talking and in his mind it is true. It is a short little hallucination (Linda really isn't in his mind), but quotes are useful for testing the water with controversial things. Here is a method to boldly put him in trance using quotes:

Y. I was reading an article the other day and it said something fun. It said that if you imagine a clock floating in the air straight in front of you, then relaxed stare at where ten o'clock would be, that you would have a light alpha brain rhythm and your mind will quiet a bit. I did it and it feels nice. Try it . . .

You now have strong brain neutral/weak trance. Though you will take him deeper with other inductions you really don't need to.

LOVE TRANCES

Believe me, this is as deep as you will ever need. Whatever you do while he is in this trance will be magnified.

Another fun use of quotes:

Y. I heard a radio talk show the other day. They were talking about how there is an inner and an outer man. The man on the show said everyone sees the outer man, but few see the emotions in a man. He went on to say that most men have huge inner selves, just waiting to be able to trust someone enough to open them. What do you think?

Checkpoints

Let's do a quick summary of what we know so far. You are seeking deep trance states where he experiences emotional pleasure. You accomplish this by checking for trance. If he isn't already where you want him get brain neutral (ex. I'd like your opinion on something...guaranteed to get any male into trance,) then lead.

You access these places deep in his mind by asking a trance question, getting him to relive some action event by describing it to you or accessing a trance that comes up in normal conversation.

You may then have him associate those deep feelings with you. Often this isn't

Craig Rovinsky

necessary, as the act of you triggering the feelings will associate them with you.

If you choose to strengthen that association it can be done with an anchor; a touch, word, or look when his emotional state peaks. He will naturally transfer a large part of his pleasant experience to the source of the experience, you. You only do this as necessary and he will fill in the rest in his mind, resulting in attraction to you.

The Biggest Danger

I repeat again, the biggest danger most women face is talking too much. Conversational hypnosis requires listening and allowing him to develop trances without you interrupting. When you are going down a trance path, your only input should be to use what he gives you to amplify his state.

Rephrasing the last few words he said, combined with the listening breath, are good conversation techniques that help control this. Hypnotic listening will create a trance state, magnifying the effectiveness.

Bluntly put, more women talk themselves out of relationships than into them. He will open to you eventually because you are the only woman who can touch his heart.

The most important thing is to be whatever you are without shame.
Rod Steiger

LOVE TRANCES

The Right Attitude

Finally, the most important thing is your attitude. It should be one of playfulness and experimentation. <u>Attach little importance to any one man. Instead begin interviewing to see who is right for you</u>. As you know now with blind luck one in five men is relationship material. When you get good at this that becomes four in five. There will still be one in five who are total zeroes but you will be able to identify them quickly.

Just follow the trance states and you will understand what you are doing. You will come up with your own methods to induce trance. It will become obvious when you are being handed trance states and trance words. It does take a little practice but once you get the hang of it you will have more personal power than you ever dreamed of.

These are the basics. As I mentioned earlier, many think that this style of hypnosis may be a bit manipulative. I think intent determines morality. If you make his life happier, beyond his wildest dreams and makes yours the same way . . . well, I think that's a very good thing.

Craig Rovinsky

What You Should Know From This Chapter

You have many tools.

V-A-K visual-auditory-kinesthetic are the three major ways a brain experiences the world.

Mirroring makes the person feel you are like them on a very primal level.

Anchoring makes the mind fire off a trance with a certain trigger; anchors don't have to be logical.

Pacing and leading encourages them into their own trances.

Quotes allow you to say things you couldn't normally, while his brain processes the information in a trance state.

Beware of too much talk, you can't listen too much.

Hypnotic Homework

This is a very easy assignment. When in conversation with someone just basically pace their rate of speech and observe the reaction. If you wish you can then speak at a

LOVE TRANCES

different rate and then switch to pacing. This will make the effect more obvious.

Craig Rovinsky

HypnoJournal

LOVE TRANCES

Unmet Needs

A basic concept of advanced conversational hypnosis is everyone has some unmet emotional need. Satisfy that need and you have them. I remember an interview with Elton John.

The crux of the interview was that Elton John felt incomplete and spent about $2½ million per month to try to feel better. The happiest moment of this hugely successful singer's life would be if someone had the ability and cared enough to go into his heart and mind.

You find out the needs with your trance language, going to core trances and trance words. Most of the time, the man will not even know he had the need. Elton John clearly has an empty space but doesn't know what to do.

Though it may sound advanced once you begin the habit of going for trance, then pursuing kinesthetically you will find these needs. When you are doing trance always keep your ears open for hints. Many people have more than one major unmet emotional need. While most people have one or two, the more unmet core emotions, the more complicated the relationship.

Unmet emotional needs frequently show up when you are doing conversation 101.

Craig Rovinsky

> When you ask what his challenges are in his job listen carefully for unmet emotional needs.

My experiences in palm reading show a few common themes in males.

Major Unmet Needs

Childhood dreams- usually are deep unrealized dreams of who they wanted to be had they not had the parents/life they were born into.

Career dreams- if he is not in his dream career this is gold.

Emotional isolation- he may never have met someone who understands him so he has isolated himself.

Physical appearance- take a physical attribute he feels self-conscious about and indirectly build him up in that area (just like a woman's concerns, he thinks this is too big or that is too small).

Adventure- he sees himself as Indiana Jones at some level... find that place in his mind/heart where that is happening.

Someone/something to idolize- he often needs a hero, usually substituting a sports star for someone in his life.

These are the areas where he can be bonded to you. For example, if you were to

LOVE TRANCES

sense he had a major unmet need in childhood you might ask, "What do you wish you had in childhood that you didn't have?" This is one of the few areas you will briefly be negative. If you feed him what he has had repressed or denied himself, he is yours.

> Compliments directed at an unmet need while he is in trance will be especially powerful.

So you've done your basic approach and want to go from here. You have his attention on you, his trance either is neutral or leaning your way, curious what will happen next. Here's how to follow up to find out most everything you'll need to know to make a decision, and what trances and trance words to use if you want to develop it further.

Be aware that just the process of going this deep in a person's mind will make them bond to you. If you decide to play with it, be careful.

Here are the next levels of trance questions. Ask them, take what you are given, pace and lead, and follow down a kinesthetic path.

Not all questions will produce gold and you wouldn't do trance language nonstop anyway. Just work it into the conversation.

85

Craig Rovinsky

In a loud bar, for example, you would be wasting your time because only bits could be heard and his focus would be distracted. However, any place where you can direct his trance and keep it is fine.

Six Magic Trance Questions

What do you want out of life?
What do you like best about your life now?
What do you deserve in life?
How would your friends describe you?
If you could be in any movie, what would it be and who would you be?
If you could star in any sport what would it be, and who would you like to be?

Not everyone will have answers to all of these. Realize that as males, we are very simple and straightforward. The questions he doesn't have an answer to tell you as much as the ones he has answers to.

Each of these questions can open up a heart and give you all you need to decide, and then act. The journey with any one of these questions could develop into hours.

Most of the time you wouldn't just ask one question after another. It just wouldn't sound right. Just memorize the basic list so you have them when you want them. Work them into the conversation singly over a

LOVE TRANCES

period of time. There are six core trances these questions access, and these trances are the basics of what makes you, you.

How about when your turn comes to answer? First, actually do the questions and honestly give yourself the answers. No one need know but you. The ones you don't want to share are the parts of your life you keep secret.

Remember, if a man doesn't have an answer he may have something he wants to keep secret, but more likely he really hasn't thought about it.

When your turn to answer comes you have two choices. If you want to build something with the two of you answer the questions using his trance words in your answer. If you have decided otherwise, make sure your answers seem to go in the opposite direction, but either way know basically what you are going to say in advance.

The lovely thing about being forty is that you can appreciate twenty-five-year-old men more.
Colleen McCullough

It is obvious that internal trances have an effect on the person's inner self. What isn't well known is these trances have noticeable, useable physical manifestations.

Try this. Ask any man what he had for breakfast. Watch where his eyes move. This

Craig Rovinsky

is where they look when they are remembering something. Later ask him something that requires him to use their imagination. Something like, "I had a dream last night and in this dream there was a giant pink gorilla wearing purple ribbons and you wouldn't believe the kind of skirt he had on . . . (pause) a ballerina's!"

You don't have to use that of course, just any question or statement that requires him to use his imagination. Watch where his eyes go.

For the vast majority of people remembered and imagined images produce opposite eye effects. You now know when he is remembering something and when he is imagining something. When he is in the imagination trance he is also in daydream trance. That's another time you can go deep into his heart with trance questions, if appropriate to the physical situation.

> Unmet needs are often satisfied in fantasy and imagination.

As you are beginning to notice, there are many, many times a person is in trance. Once you learn to recognize those times and select the trances you want to work with you will realize you really don't have to induce trance states. You can just wait. Every man

LOVE TRANCES

will give you everything you need to know if you just know what trances to go for.

How to Hypnotize a Rich Man

Say you are interested in a man who just happens to be rich. It is easy to find the unmet needs of people with great accomplishments.

<u>All you need to do is remove their accomplishment and find out what kind of person they think they are without it.</u>

For a rich man it might be something like, "Everyone knows you because of your money. If you didn't have money, what do you think people would find out about you they don't know now?"

Remove their accomplishment and find out who they believe they are without it. Easy. Gold. (Of course, by now you know to have him in trance when you ask the question don't you?)

This brings up the question, "Is it worth it to marry for money?" I have had many palm reading clients who have done this. They all seemed unhappy at a core level. That isn't to say a marriage based on money might not work, but it is more likely you will end up feeling like a sleazy hooker.

Craig Rovinsky

Sex and Hypnosis

Let's talk about sex and hypnosis. As a woman physical attractiveness is one of your unmet needs, but this is in your head. As a woman you don't need hypnosis to get sex. The answer to "does he want to have sex with me?" is yes.

Remember earlier I mentioned a client who had read a study about how one of five men wanted a different woman each night. She told me of another study in the article where attractive men and women each approached members of the opposite sex and asked about several potential social activities.

The result that concerns us here is that three of four men actually did agree to have sex with a woman they just met. By the way, no women agreed to sex with men they just met.

I bring this up because in my experience as a palm reader I have never seen a woman happy with the way she looks. A woman could be a bikini model, causing car accidents as she walks down the street and she'll be wondering if her ears are fat.

Personally, I like sex and I don't care what a man thinks of me as long as I get what I want from him—which is usually sex.
Valerie Perrine

LOVE TRANCES

The point is you are sexy to most men just as you are. Feelings that you are not physically attractive are in your own head.

You know the difference between good sex and great sex? Good sex ends with, "I love you." Great sex ends with, "Are you OK?"
A palmistry client

Earlier I mentioned that advertisers use hypnosis. One of the biggest trances they have is their marketed idea of what a woman should look like. For decades advertising has associated feeling wonderful with looking a certain way. It's no coincidence that to feel better about a problem you didn't know you had you need to buy their product.

The pressure on women to look a certain way or feel unattractive is probably the biggest abuse of hypnosis in recent history. Once you start seeing the ads and recognizing the hypnotic inductions, the trance music, and the transfer of emotions you will begin to realize you've been had.

It's time for you to decide if you are beautiful, not someone who wants to sell you something.

The legs aren't so beautiful, I just know what to do with them.
Marlene Dietrich

Craig Rovinsky

Trust me when I say that 99% of women are beautiful and sensual just as they are. They just don't know it. You are in that 99%.

The 17 Million Dollar Induction

If you watch TV cop shows you may have seen a show about a Brink's armored car robbery. The take was 17 million dollars. The curious thing about this particular robbery was the man who did all the risky work gave just about all of the money (except for about $50,000) to the woman and her accomplices who just waited outside. Why? Without knowing it, she was triggering one of his unmet needs.

When police investigated they knew who did the robbery itself and found several pages on his beeper during the time of the robbery. Over and over the pages read 143...143...143. Only after they busted everyone in the group did they find out what that meant.

The guy who actually stole the money was in love with the woman. She was playing him totally. Though they never had sex he was totally obsessed with her. To keep him going during the robbery she kept sending him the numbers 143. The numbers stood for the number of letters in each word of the phrase, "I love you."

LOVE TRANCES

Why was this so effective? He was in an intense emotional state during the robbery, compounded by his love for her. When he received the numbers in this brain state he had to translate them in his mind to the words they stood for.

There was no time for conscious thought of his actions as the induction was repeated over and over, each repetition magnifying the earlier ones, an old stage hypnotist's secret. Though I seriously doubt this woman had any idea why this worked, it did work. Interviews with the man in prison showed he still has no idea what hit him.

Action is the antidote to despair.
Joan Baez

Craig Rovinsky

What You Should Know From This Chapter

Keep it fun.

Do not attach too much importance to any one man.

Find his unmet emotional needs.

Compliments directed at an unmet emotional need while he is in trance will be especially powerful.

Hypnotic Homework

Listen for unmet emotional needs in people. Consider how you can use that information to create love.

LOVE TRANCES

HypnoJournal

Craig Rovinsky

LOVE TRANCES

Naturally Occurring Trances

Right after a person picks up the phone they are often in neutral trance and are open to imprinting or leading into other more useful trances. The act of talking on the phone is usually done while in a type of trance. Phone salesmen market this way because it pays.

Another naturally occurring trance moment is on the "down-side" of a laugh. The laugh will build to a peak and rapidly decline. Just as the laugh begins to decline is a wonderful time to make a request or plant a thought. Laughter is a state all its own.

Really, in terms of importance, laughter should have its own book. There just isn't that much to it. When someone laughs, they end up in total brain neutral. The logical mind may have been used to get the joke, but the laughter is a completely unconscious act and comes from a different part of the brain.

> The few moments after a laugh peaks the mind is wide open.

Craig Rovinsky

Anything you say to him at that point will be taken in deeply and its impact magnified. This is a very good time for any compliment you may have prepared, or for any power words to be used. Let's say you know one of his power words is "alive."

H. Laughs hard at something, and starts to come down from the peak of the laugh.
Y. Laughing with him, "You make me feel so alive!"

This doesn't read as great guns but you have to try it. Prepare a few things you want to imprint in him, and wait. When he laughs use the most appropriate one. If none fit, use what he either just gave you that he is laughing about, or just wait for another time.

> There will be an endless supply of laugh opportunities. Most laughter doesn't happen in response to a joke. Laughter is basically a social act. People laugh about things that aren't funny all the time. Be aware that a laugh will frequently come out of nowhere.

If you are with someone who doesn't laugh easily, look twice. This is just a personal feeling, but I have always felt those

LOVE TRANCES

that laugh easily tend to be a lot more fun to be around.

If you want to get the timing on laughter trance, watch a nationally produced commercial. There are several that make you laugh. The better ones will deliver the sales message just as the laugh is coming down. It is in that moment the trance occurs. Try the laughter trance. It is very easy, just prepare what you want to imprint. Here is how I once used it.

I worked at a job where I wanted the afternoon off. My supervisor, Jessie, was talking to a group of people. I sat in the conversation and just waited for her to laugh (it doesn't take long until Jessie laughs, she's nice.) As her laugh began to subside I asked, "It's really slow, can I go home?" She went quiet for a moment, a smile still on her face from the laugh, and said "sure."

By the way, if you ask someone to do something for you and they go quiet don't say a word, no matter what. <u>The longer they are quiet the greater chance you will get your request.</u> They are inside in a trance state, don't interrupt it or you will engage their logical minds.

Beauty is in the eye of the beholder, and it may be necessary from time to time to give a stupid or misinformed beholder a black eye.
Miss Piggy

Craig Rovinsky

Road Hypnosis: Powerful and Dangerous

Another somewhat dangerous natural trance occurs while someone is driving. Have you ever noticed how easy it can be to open up to someone when it is just the two of you driving down the road? You have heard of "road hypnosis." It is literally a trance induced by the repetitive nature of driving, the centerline of the road creating a strobe-like effect, white line, no line, white line, no line, over and over. After a while you get lulled into total absorption, into trance.

Questions asked when in road trance can be quite effective, especially if they involve him projecting into the future. Wait until he gets that "look" while driving, on a deserted freeway (doing this in any traffic is asking for trouble,) then ask your future-paced question. He gets a future trance nested in a road hypnosis trance.

Car accidents are quite possible at this moment.

Be very aware of what is happening. He will be gone deep inside in his mind. If you use this, do it somewhere very safe and keep your eyes on the road as well. If it goes deep rapidly tell him, "… hold that thought…" pull over and retrigger the trance by asking, "… you were saying…?" and listen.

LOVE TRANCES

Million Dollar Trances for Free

Recall the earlier discussions about television commercials, how they create a brain state and at the end of the commercial plug their product. The advertisers literally spend millions to find out exactly how to put your brain in exactly the right trance for the message.

This is most easily noticed on sports ads. Some income comes from ticket sales but the bulk of the income of sports comes from TV advertising. All that money to pay insane salaries comes from powerful advertising that produces wide-open trance states, ready for imprinting.

Watch your boy-toy closely as he watches advertisements on television. Notice which ads produce the strongest trances in him. When those ads come on again, prepare to usurp the trance for your own use. Just a second before the advertiser plugs their product, plug your product—<u>you</u>!

You might future pace, compliment on an unmet need, hand squeeze and look in his eyes, or just hit a couple trance words in an off-handed comment.

Jeanine watched as her friend tranced to a sports car commercial. As the trance peaked near the end she asked if he ever dreamed about just driving cross-country for a while. The next few hours went by as minutes as he told her of his dream trip. He

Craig Rovinsky

now tells friends that it was that night he fell in love with her.

Television is a trance-induction device that takes second place to none. You can be handed many powerful trances if you just watch him closely. After you get accomplished at timing thirty-second commercial trances you can expand to using trance states generated by longer shows.

The Out to Lunch Trance

Another trance you will often be handed is the far away look. You know the picture. The mall's open, but the stores are all closed. When you notice this state, use the phrase, ". . . a penny for your thoughts." This phrase is hardwired into many to produce some verbal response. Since you are doing it when they are in trance the power is greatly magnified.

About half the time nothing will happen as far as response goes. About half the time they will open up on something you never expected, and it will usually be some core trance. This is a frequent freebie so if you let an opportunity slip by don't worry. People are spacing out all the time. There will be another chance very soon.

The Magic of Ultradian Rhythms

Most of the time when someone has that "out to lunch" look it is because they are

LOVE TRANCES

experiencing the trance cycle of their ultradian rhythm. So what is an ultradian rhythm? It's a mini-nap your brain takes periodically by going into a brain-neutral trance. People think they just space out at random, but it is a regular cycle. It happens to everyone.

Your brain takes about a ten to twenty-minute break every ninety minutes or so. It's not uncommon for that cycle to go to one break every 120 minutes. There is some variation between people, but these are the basic guidelines you should start with.

Observe the person of your desire. Watch for the "out to lunch" look. When you see it note the time. At around the seventy-five to ninety-minute mark start watching again. When he trances again note the time. You want to repeat this again, as trance can come from many things and you are looking for ultradian rhythms. When you see it again, note the time.

If it is about the same you have the timing for that man's ultradian rhythms. You can now predict when he will naturally trance and can decide what you want to do when he does. For most people, this cycle is constant from day to day. If he trances for ten minutes once every eighty minutes it's safe to think that his timing will basically remain so on future days. Just check every so often, in case he his having a different kind of day.

Craig Rovinsky

> The ultradian rhythm trance produces a soft, gentle trance. This trance is ideal for gift giving. If you have a present, wait until he goes into his ultradian trance and he will respond more emotionally.

The Confusion Trance

Confusion is another naturally occurring trance. The mind is wide open, seeking for anything to give it order and meaning. You must be very careful using the confusion trance. Confusion is easily experienced as a negative feeling. Still, it is powerful enough so you should be aware of it. Here is my personal story of a confusion trance.

Many, many years ago I met a woman at a beach party (nowhere near as beautiful as my wife, you understand). We spent most of that evening together and I let her know when and where I worked. Well, it so happened that the moment she chose to walk by the next day I was visiting with another friend, let's call him Goran. For reasons still unknown he took an instant dislike to her, but I hadn't realized it yet.

She asked me if I would like to go to a picnic and I said yes. Goran, in a powerful voice from out of the blue voice said, "No, you don't want to." It came on so strong I was shocked. I stared at him with a dumb

LOVE TRANCES

look and said the brilliant, "Huh?" He repeated firmly, "You don't want to go out with her." I turned to her and said, "I guess I don't." For some reason, she never came by after that.

Frankly, for years I couldn't figure out why I reacted that way. When you ask a volunteer in a stage hypnotism show why he did what he did, he will often reply he knew what he was doing, he just couldn't help himself. It was years later when I discovered the confusion trance that it came together.

Goran's first powerful, "No, you don't want to," put me in brain neutral. I wasn't expecting that and stood confused, my brain wide open waiting to find meaning. His second statement had the same power as a stage hypnotist's command, and worked exactly the same. It's a good thing he didn't know what he was doing or I might have ended up clucking like a chicken.

Confusion trances are a little touchy. Overall, you might want to stay away from them, but it is good to be aware just in case you have something you are wondering how to install and the natural course of the day puts him in a confusion trance. Who are you to deny the natural course of things? Use the trance and install what you want. To deliberately use confusion trance can backfire, though. It's just too easy for a brain to take confusion as negative. That is not the kind of thing you want to link to yourself.

105

Craig Rovinsky

How Was Your Day?

Once you know someone's trance words you can prepare a nice surprise. Open with, "How was your day?" If you are handed pleasure trances you will, of course, amplify them and associate them with you. Sometimes though the answer to this is neutral or a bit down. Here is where you go to work.

Have prepared a description of your day that includes his trance words and trance states (that you experienced during the day, of course). It is extra strong when they have had a lackluster day and you appear to make them feel alive in just the right way. If their energy is low from being tired start gently and build it up. It is a strong bonding trance.

Take a Trip and Never Leave the Farm

Being tired is another physical state that leads to conscious brain shutdown and trance. When someone is tired, for all practical purposes they are in brain neutral.

This is the perfect time to look into their eyes and ask, "If you had a magic wand that would take this all away and let you go on any vacation, where would you go?"

Once they start talking amplify this like you've never amplified before. Ask what an

LOVE TRANCES

ideal day would be like. Ask what they would be doing and if in the description he doesn't give feelings, ask what he would be feeling. When you get to a hot action/feeling go with the three-deep, taking them deeper into the experience.

If you can, have him close his eyes at that point and describe to you what is taking place in his fantasy vacation. The only thing that's missing is if he acted it out on stage, but let's not go there. You are going to generate incredible pleasure states that he will associate with you.

These states are even stronger because of the contrast from tired to pleasure, and being tired gives you the trance to begin talking about the vacation. Powerful, powerful stuff. Sweet.

Everybody Trances

Let me give you an example of a naturally occurring trance I experienced.

I was at a taco stand waiting in line and I noticed a very pretty woman sitting in a booth. Simple lines, dark hair and a flowery summer dress, she was the beautiful girl-next-door type. I also noticed she was totally entranced by me.

To be blunt she couldn't take her eyes off me, looking me up and down with obvious lust. Of course I could understand her fascination and enjoyed it! Suddenly the plot

Craig Rovinsky

changed as she looked at me, smiled and began to get up to approach me. That's when she whipped out the white cane with the red tip.

LOVE TRANCES

What You Should Know From This Chapter

There are many naturally occurring trances.

They are characterized by total absorption with narrow focus.

They happen predictably, so once you know what trance you will get and when to expect it, you can plan for it.

Hypnotic Homework

Observe someone while they are watching a commercial. Watch for the trance look and notice when in the commercial it happens. Also notice what commercial it was. Soon you will know exactly when you can expect him to be in trance and can consider what you would like to do with that trance.

Craig Rovinsky

HypnoJournal

LOVE TRANCES

Trance Magnifiers

Now let's get to the next level. Let's start with a few empowering concepts and begin to look at this from an advanced perspective.

The most important thing is to keep this fun. The lighter you make this inside yourself, the more you turn it into an adventure, the better your results will be.

You will see the inner workings of strange men, shallow men, dangerous men, and some that are just right for you. You will be able to make emotional connections with those you want and suddenly your opportunities become greatly enhanced.

The best attitude for most of this is playfulness, as it is the best attitude for most of life. Don't take it too seriously and don't get attached to any one result or any one person. It's not famine time anymore for you in romance, it's time to start interviewing and see who is up to it.

I repeat, do not attach too much importance to any one person! You give away most of your hypnotic power if you come from the place of neediness. Fun is the heart space where you should live your romantic life.

Let me give you an example so strong and blatant it is considered brainwashing by many.

111

Craig Rovinsky

Brainwashing 101

Some people consider the "Moonies", members of the Unification Church of Rev. Moon of South Korea, to be a brainwashing cult. Many years ago I got lost and wandered into a Moonie drop-in center in New York City. It was a small place called "The Heart of the Big Apple."

Sure enough, I was invited to a lecture, then to a weekend retreat. It was at this retreat I experienced the powerful effects of bypassing the critical faculty.

On the first day there we were assigned a mentor who was to show us around. Mine was a very nice woman named Faith. She said she was from Minneapolis, MN, and was a walking example of love that any religion would have been proud to show as one of their own. Love, love, love. Love bombing. Delightfully, blissfully overwhelming, and one of the best tools they had was a little thing called a "choo-choo."

We formed a circle with ten to twenty people, the larger the better. We held hands, smiling our little heads off. Knowing what emotion was about to overtake us always put everyone in a great mood. Then, while looking in the eyes of your guide (or whomever) we began to chant together.

"Choo-choo-choo-choo-choo-choo-yea-yea-pow!" The held hands would pump with every other choo, and the chant grew with

LOVE TRANCES

enthusiasm until when we hit the "POW" we all punched our held hands into the air, got this incredible rush of pleasure and felt massive, peaceful love for each other. I only did it a few times in one weekend, in 1980. I'll carry it with me the rest of my life.

Why? Well, the patterns of brainwashing, military, political, or religious, are the same. What happens inside your mind is very predictable. When you enter a trance state, in this case by chanting, your brain triggers a burst of cortical excitation. This is your "Aha!" section of the brain.

You don't have to get him to chant. This is a common state when a man's favorite sports team scores. Any deep excitement trance will trigger this cortical output. You naturally feel an attraction for the source of this primal feeling, the other person. You also instinctively bond with the source of this rush.

You get Aha, rapport, bonding. Just like any pleasure, this is chocolate to the brain and you find yourself desiring more of this feeling and more of this person who is giving this to you. This brain sequence has built many religions and many empires. It is plenty strong for creating love in as many people as you like.

Craig Rovinsky

Hypnotize His Secrets Out of Him

Let me introduce you to an advanced concept I call a nested trance. It is very good for getting out secrets. Remember, when you quote someone the person listening has to create an imaginary person in their mind to represent who you are talking about. If that person then told a story it would require another level of imagery, a trance within a trance. When a person is experiencing these nested trances their inner responses are amplified.

Here's an example. Say you have been seeing someone. He has possibilities, but you are wondering if he is a cheater.

Earlier we talked about asking a guy his opinion to get trance. Start off with, "I would like your opinion on something." Pause. He will be in brain neutral. He's waiting so he can give you his opinion and at some level in his mind he is already fantasizing about sounding intelligent or being right. It's a guy thing.

Asking for a guy's opinion and pausing is a sure way to get trance.

"I have a friend Lori, (short pause), and she has a boyfriend George, (pause, now his brain is processing an image within an

114

LOVE TRANCES

image), and she is wondering if he is playing her."

Pause here, don't stare at him directly but watch and feel for strong responses. If the thought hasn't even occurred to him to stray he will remain in brain neutral waiting for your next statement, or offer positive advice. Otherwise guilty, stray, or inappropriate thoughts will be greatly magnified.

I can't describe it to you, but when you see it you will know. Most often it appears as confusion. This is one of the few times you will deliberately use a confusion trance. Give it a couple seconds and continue.

"I was wondering what you think she should do." You have to play it by ear, but his answer, by its feel, should confirm what you sensed in the first pause. It's difficult to describe, but after you do this you will understand, as it will jump right out at you.

By creating a deep trance within a trance state, then hitting with the key question confusion in his mind is created. If he needs to process information of his own straying before he answers it will be obvious. His mind is taken up with processing the image within an image and he gets confused. Obviously, if he has nothing to hide his trance wouldn't change significantly.

A palm reading client once told me, "You want to know if he's married? If he puts on a condom without being asked, he's married."

Craig Rovinsky

A more practical clue is if he won't give you his home phone number.

Psychic Hypnosis

This technique is the secret of a gigolo I once knew. He told me his clients wanted two things and one of them was a good listener. His method for this used a mind trick for him, and a silent technique for her. He called it "psychic hypnosis."

In his own mind he would convince himself that the woman sitting across from him was this fascinating celebrity. By making this real in his mind his genuine fascination would affect her in a beautiful way.

> Being the center of someone's riveted attention, being listened to thoughtfully and with genuine interest and caring creates an instant bond and trance.

The stronger he hypnotized himself that she was a celebrity the stronger the effect on her, and as he became genuinely more and more fascinated by her she began to feel like a queen.

To amplify the trance, he did nothing. Specifically, he would always wait a full three seconds after she had finished talking before

LOVE TRANCES

he would say a word. Since he was fascinated by her he was in a listening heart space and she could sense that. She would fill the silence with more of her emotions.

An important point is that while listening to her he wasn't busy thinking about what he was going to say next. Being fascinated by her allowed him to do this. Face it, when you can't wait for the other person to quit talking so you can say something, they can tell.

If you master nothing else, master the technique of silent hypnosis for listening, with the three-second pause. My friend makes half of a very nice living with this.

Bill Clinton, a man who has much in common with a gigolo, is a master of this. Love him or hate him, he has mastered the ability of totally focusing on the person he is with to the extent that they feel like they are the only person in the world. In person Bill Clinton is incredibly charming, and this is the reason why.

Time Distortion and Commitment

Time distortion is good but you must be careful and use it only at the right time. Before going into how and when I want to take a side trip and talk about time.

Time is not a thing; it is a mental concept our brains use to organize memories. The only real time is now. What your mind thinks is time are mental constructions of past

Craig Rovinsky

memories and future dreams. There may be some nice philosophical arguments on the nature of time, but in the real world this is how it appears in your mind. Since time is a mental construction, it is variable within the individual.

Time can be slow or fast. If you are listening to a boring lecture, as far as your brain is concerned, it really does take forever. If you are reading someone who fascinates you then time can just fly by. You can use this principle, but first a warning.

For some men a powerful negative trance word is "relationship" or anything that rings that bell. Any word like that he needs to say first. His deep emotional trances will start to go off every time he sees you, so he will.

Time distortion, if used too early, will trigger his fears of the "r" word. You use time distortion when you know you already have him leaning strongly to the "r" word.

> To use time distortion, talk about a future event that the two of you either are doing together, or will have some common connection to.

You do this, of course, when you have him in brain neutral or trance. This is a very good time to use some of his trance words. Remember, "conversation" at a moment

LOVE TRANCES

when he is in trance will be perceived as real.

He will process the idea that the two of you extend into the future. In his mind it will be processed as his version of a relationship. Hopefully, by now you know what he thinks that is.

The secret is the timing. A little too late is better than too early. Remember, brain state precedes all other factors. Don't try to run a conversational trance process on him without having him in trance first.

STOP

The word "stop" is a great trance induction. What would it be like if you were to stop...

And wonder how you could use that pause in your brain after it hears the word "stop."

Hypnotize Him With His Dreams

Remember Martin Luther King's, "I have a dream" speech? For many people it is all they know of his speeches. The theme of dreams is that strong. All you need to do is get him to tell you about one of his dreams.

I don't think I need to mention that if it is a bad dream cut it off, or if he won't shut up at least link the negative trance to his old girlfriend (that slut.) Something like, "Gee, that is a horrible, putrid, festering emotion .

119

Craig Rovinsky

. . it's kind of like the feeling around your old girlfriend."

Whenever someone is in a nasty trance be very careful about touching them. Only if you are certain it will comfort them it is the right thing to do. It is too easy to bond those emotions with you with a touch. Save the touch for good emotions, unless you are sure it will be comforting to them. Then it is good.

Anyway . . . let's assume it's a good dream. When someone describes back to you a dream they had they go into trance. It is more than brain neutral; it is a nice accessible trance.

One possibility here is the revelation of solid gold trance words. Words leaned on here come from deep in his subconscious. This is a very easy trance to use . . .as he is winding down but still "dreamy," just say something like, "That reminds me . . ." Go on to what you want to imprint. Using the power words he gave you in the dream state will make this especially strong.

The Magic Questions Game

A number of psychological games are floating about. These are wonderful for getting trances, trance words, and revelations. You ask him the questions then tell him you will share with him your answers. You, of course, prepare your answers so you just have to focus on

LOVE TRANCES

whether you want to match his trances in your answers.

Here is one version I learned in high school in the 1970's, though any simple personality test from a magazine can be used, as long as it asks for positive answers.

What is your favorite color?
What is your favorite animal?
You are at the beach on a beautiful day. The sun is out, the sand is warm and the surf is gently pounding. What do you do?

With every answer, take it further. For example if their favorite color is violet ask them what it makes them feel. Always, always, drive for the kinesthetic. If they feel especially talkative let 'em fly. Take it as deep as you can, then when you feel the emotion starting to come down from the peak move on to the next subject.

The Secret Meanings of the Questions

The favorite color is your view of yourself. The favorite animal is how your friends see you. The beach represents their thoughts on sensuality/sexuality. This is a very fun trance inducing game with much potential to give you what you need to know and people love to play it. Try it once, there is almost nothing to learn and you will amaze yourself

121

Craig Rovinsky

how many trance states and words people cheerfully will give you.

Stacking Realities

Stacking realities is another nice way to magnify trance. It is basically a pace-and-lead induction.

> You comment on three things that they can easily verify, and then lead them into the emotion you want.

As you find yourself reading this, noticing each word, and wondering what is next, you find yourself realizing you have the personal power to trigger the emotions you want in men.

You can also stack realities with three articles, or three anything followed by what you want to lead them into. You are making his mind go yes, yes, yes three times silently, and then taking it where you want. Silent agreement is much easier to get than verbal agreement.

Universal Trance Inductions

Certain types of communication access trance states. Any communication that causes someone to experience physical or

LOVE TRANCES

emotional sensations, real or remembered, gets them to imagine a picture of some kind, uses poetic or storytelling language, or goes to the core of who they are will reliably produce trance.

Most of the time the best trance work is to let him talk. When he hands you one of his preexisting trance states, run with it. Sometimes he won't be talkative. When you need to carry the conversation you always want to be thinking about bringing him to a pleasurable, kinesthetic trance state. When you tell your stories structure them as follows and they become inductions.

1-2-3 Conversational Induction Structure

1. Initial induction
2. Deepen trance
3. Link to you

Assume he is into downhill ski racing:

Initial induction: I was watching a men's downhill race the other day. Isn't it great how wonderful you can feel just watching ski racing?

Expand trance:It's like you are almost there, battling the mountain. It's as if every adventure you've ever had

123

Craig Rovinsky

squeezed into a whole series of timeless moments.

Linking the trance to you:Something like that makes me feel so alive, too!

Learn the structure that take a story and change it to a hypnotic induction. The link seems simple because most of it is automatic, though the link isn't necessary if you can see he clearly views you as the source of his feelings. If it isn't clear link with above or something like, "I see you feel it too" and go with what ever comes.

LOVE TRANCES

What You Should Know From This Chapter

Trances can be deepened and magnified.

Certain types of communication create and deepen trances.

Silent agreement deepens trance.

Hypnotic Homework

Learn the structure to make a conversation hypnotic. Practice it, then when you get the opportunity, create and deepen a trance. Give him a delicious emotional experience.

Craig Rovinsky

HypnoJournal

LOVE TRANCES

A Ph.D. in Loveology

Before you get to this level, you should be well practiced on the basics. It isn't as important to memorize specific trances, as it is to be able to work with whatever trances they give you. It isn't really hard. By now you have much of his core trance structure. You should know several core trances before you proceed.

> The techniques in this chapter are meant to be used with someone who you have something emotional already. They will have limited impact with someone new, but can cement love if it has already started.

You should know the most important things in his life, and at least the first three in order of priority. You also need to know what challenges he faces and what he believes his possibilities are. You should also know how he knows when he is succeeding at meeting his own beliefs about his core identity. To him, how does he know when he is succeeding at life?

This is the first level of advanced hypnotic bonding. Just working with the core identity trances will bond most people quite deeply.

127

Craig Rovinsky

Here I am going to hide one of the best secrets in the book. It is a little one-line induction magnifier. He's going down a trance path, talking about something that makes him very animated. You simply ask him, "What is it about ＿＿＿ that makes it important to who you are?" He will hand you gold.

Of course he doesn't have to be animated, just in any deep state you want to magnify. The phrase, ". . . makes it important to you . . ." can be "challenges you," "makes it what you want to be," whatever is appropriate to what he has given you. Memorize this and use it.

Anchoring for Life

Remember anchoring? When you really want to anchor something here are the big guns. While most anchors become stronger with repetition, these three power anchors will usually take strongly the first time. If you do it powerfully, they will be imprinted for life.

Anchoring in His Home

The first major-league anchor is to anchor items in his home to you. Only do one or two items. You accomplish this by finding out what knick-knacks he has that are important to him. As he is telling the stories, you want to be listening for items that bring

LOVE TRANCES

him into a trance state that you want. When you find an item that meets your needs you listen. As he starts to wind down, ask him, "Can I hold it?" You must ask permission to hold the item. If he says no, respect that. Most of the time you get a yes.

Now, with him watching, you hold it and look at it. You describe what it makes you feel, using the trance words he just gave you when he talked about it. Just repeat them back in the same order, like we did in the basics. In this situation, though, you are going to get the benefit of all the emotions he has in the item, transferred to you.

> H. Talks about item and gives you trance words of power, gentleness, and peace, over the course of a five-minute talk about his favorite knick-knack.
> Y. [holding and gazing at item) I know what you mean. This color blue is powerful and gentle at the same time. It does make you feel peaceful, doesn't it? [Of course as you see the emotion grow in him again, you touch the back of his hand and look into his eyes briefly. You know the look).

From now on, whenever he looks at that item it will remind him of both his great emotions associated with it, and you. Since it is in his home, he will notice it, and you, on a subconscious level many times each day.

129

Craig Rovinsky

(As long as you are in his home, don't forget his bookshelf. His books are the map of his mind).

Anchor the Stars

The second major anchor is to anchor the stars to you. Any major physical thing he sees is fine, but the stars work exceptionally well. When out on a nighttime walk eventually the mood will become romantic. When he is feeling an emotional peak, squeeze his hand, look up at the stars with him and say, "Look at the stars . . . it's almost as if our love was the same energy as the stars." Continue to gaze for as long as he does.

I remember a presidential debate between Walter Mondale and Ronald Reagan. Reagan was telling one of his stories. He was talking about driving along the California coast, just having a nice drive, and he began to look at the stars. He paused, totally tranced. Just the memory of gazing at the stars years ago put him in deep trance.

He completely forgot what he was talking about. When he realized he was totally spaced on live national TV he babbled something to finish the answer and went on. Stars are strong trance magic.

LOVE TRANCES

> A very similar anchor is the moon. It is especially good for long-distance relationships, as you can anchor over the phone while both looking at the same moon. Many palm reading clients have told me of this being quite effective.

Anchor White

The third major anchor is to anchor something to the color white. Anything you want to have him experience in a massive way anchor to white. Bring him to peak trance, and use one of his most powerful trance words to describe how this feeling is really like the color white. Fire the anchor once saying something like, "I was reading how some colors go with some emotions. Look, as you look at that pure white, how we feel strong (his trance word). It feels like love with adventure (his trance words) doesn't it?"

The Invisible You-We Shift

I used a useful language pattern in that example, the "you-we." I used "you" when talking about the feeling of white, and used "we" talking about how it can be felt now. You will never be caught doing this shift and

Craig Rovinsky

it causes him to associate those feelings to you.

Life shrinks or expands in proportions to one's courage.
Anais Nin

How to Hypnotize a Sports Junkie

Though not a core anchor because it doesn't apply to all men, if one of the men you are considering is extremely into a particular sports team, use the sports anchor. I taught this idea to one client who was having trouble getting her boyfriend to commit. Sound familiar? He was obsessed with the Green Bay Packers. Her solution was very original.

When is a guy in a deep, deep trance? When he thinks he is going to get sex. His thought patterns are very focused. His mind is very open, anxious to say anything, do anything. I'm sure you've had this experience. Knowing this, she was dressed in blue jeans with a Green Bay Packer's Jersey. As they started to play around a bit the emotions grew.

When things started to get more than warm she stopped, looked him in the eyes and whispered, "We have a Green Bay Packer love." She paused, he looked at her glassy-eyed and said, "That's exactly what it is." Decorum prohibits me telling what I

LOVE TRANCES

think the rest of that story was, she wouldn't tell me. I do know this. They are now married, with a baby.

> Once you already have a good connection with a sports junkie, hypnotize him to associate his sports emotions to sex with you.

Hypnotize Him With Just a Touch

The solar plexus bypass is a physical way to bypass conscious resistance. It is a physical trance induction. We have word-feelings in our head brain but for most of us our emotional experiences happen in the body. The base of the body's emotional brain is right around the solar plexus. If you have someone who says one thing but you know feels another here is what to do.

As he is slowing down talking use the simplest state interrupt. "Stop . . . your brain says that (pointing to his head) but what does it say right here (run your finger down and gently touch him in the solar plexus)?" He will get a trance look. Do not say a word here. Just wait as long as it takes until he starts talking. You can take it from here. You must be careful, though.

Use this only if you are quite certain of the outcome you desire and want to lock it

133

Craig Rovinsky

in. If he comes out with something else as a feeling from the solar plexus, that will be perceived as being absolutely true also and will lock in. If you are not certain what he will say, you are gambling. The solar plexus bypass can do wonders and can backfire horribly.

The Heart Space Induction

The last trance work we will look at here is based on the ideas expressed by many therapists in several types of therapy. The concept is we experience emotions physically, in specific parts of our body. You will be creating a separate place in his emotional body and assigning it to you.

For most people who are in love, if you were to ask them where they feel it when they think about the one they love it will be a specific location.

> Once you assign a location to someone else they then become part of you.

The first step is you must create a place in his body and link it to you. This is easy once you have pet names for each other. If you do this is simple, if not adapt to his personal trance words that express strong feelings toward you.

LOVE TRANCES

Y. You know how we have special names for each other?

H. Yea, I really like thinking of you as my little rose muffin.

Y. When you think of me like that, where do you feel it?

H. Touches himself (probably around the solar plexus, but wherever is fine).

Y. When I think of you I feel it right here (indicate where you really do feel it).

Tell me, if you were to imagine a soft energy beam connecting those two parts of us, what color would it be?

H. Violet, a soft powerful beam that goes back and forth.

Y. Wow! I asked you this because last night I had a dream where we were just our two special names, floating in space, and we were attached by a violet beam of light (or together in a violet bubble). It is so fascinating you said violet. Why violet?

H. To me, violet reminds me of the movie, "The Color Purple" where Whoopi Goldberg's character ended up being loved unconditionally. Love did win in the end.

Y. That's fascinating. So purple means unconditional love? Well, I'll keep our purple connection alive if you will . . .

Craig Rovinsky

H... smiles, fade to romantic music . . .

This example is a strong body trance. The connection with energy is a very good idea. Combined with a dream trance it is almost irresistible. The other thing to notice is now you have an emotional location in his body assigned to you.

In the second step you create a special place in his mind/body and assign it to you. You mention that you read an interesting article on relaxation and would he be interested in learning how to relax?

You sit or lay him down and get him to brain neutral. You talk about how we put different pictures in our minds in different places. Ask him to think of his Mother (or any generic positive thing). Ask him if he were to imagine where in his mind that picture was, where would it be?

Most men are strongly visual, so you can just work with picture locations, otherwise just ask them to imagine where the thought would be and adapt from there. He will indicate a location. Nest ask him to imagine something from when he was a kid, like being a fireman.

You are looking for something that was positive but doesn't mean much anymore. Ask him where that picture is. Most men will indicate an area in the back right region of their brain. If he is different just go with it. Now, just point out that the two pictures

LOVE TRANCES

were in different parts. Then say, "Next . . .." pause.

"If you were to imagine a place in your mind of perfect love, perfect peace, (whatever his most powerful trance words are for love) where would that be?" You may have to wait for this. If he can't come up with anything ask him just to imagine where it is. You now must link it to you.

Without directly mentioning the energy beam you will use the color from the first step. In our example it was violet. You ask him to now imagine this entire special spot is surrounded and protected by a soft violet light. Ask him to imagine this soft violet light, working with it in his imagination until he can feel its energy.

I don't think much explanation is needed here. If you want, you can go further by telling him anytime he needs to go inside himself he can just connect with you on your violet beam of energy, from you to him.

You want to have experience doing trance before you try this. It takes a little talent, but not much. You probably will not be able to accomplish this as your first trance work out of the book, nor should you.

The key is to recognize the trance flow and work with the trance words and states he gives you. Practice with examples, but understand what is going on in his mind. It then is very easy to hypnotize him using his own trances with the specific application

Craig Rovinsky

depending on what you plan for him in your life.

The United States military recruiters are great sources of this type of trance language. Pamphlets and websites are filled with inductions that remake your view of yourself. Study them and apply their inductions to your own use. I have an U.S. Marine Corp pamphlet designed to recruit women. Here is an excerpt...

Where is that girl that lived in your mind?

Quite often you wanted to be more like her.

She was ponytails to your barrettes.

An A-minus to your B-plus.

When you threw like a girl, she threw harder.

She went by your name and followed you everywhere.

Once upon a time, there was this girl. She had an attitude. And a spirit nobody could tame. She was tough and attacked each new day without fear. She went by your name and spoke with a voice only you could hear. She lived in your mind.

Find her!

LOVE TRANCES

Taking Out the Trash With Hypnosis

So, by now you may have played with trance work and found out it is stronger than you thought possible. Trouble is, now you have some reject head over heels in love with you and you can't seem to lose him. Vowing to be more careful in the future with your powers you wonder how to undo what you have done. It is simple, in most cases.

Remember core trances? Find out what his deepest core trances are, and disagree with them in some way. He will be shocked and amazed and want nothing to do with you. He will leave with the words, "I thought I knew you."

In the next section we will discuss some useful hallucinations that will make your life better. Remember, everyone, including you and I, goes in and out of trance on a regular basis. By choosing a few tasty hallucinations you can empower yourself to become the romance heroine in your own life in a very short time.

Craig Rovinsky

What You Should Know From This Chapter

The three super-anchors are items in his home, the stars, and the color white.

The solar plexus bypass can induce trance.

You can create a space in his heart that is just for you.

Hypnotic Homework

This will be your first bit of slightly advanced homework. What I want you to do is go back and reread the solar plexus bypass section. Make sure you understand it because it may be a bit before you have the right opportunity.

When you are sure you have him wanting to do something but not admitting it, that's when you use it.

You need to be sure he is already leaning the way you want to go, but once you do you can use this to get him to commit. Be ready.

LOVE TRANCES

HypnoJournal

Craig Rovinsky

LOVE TRANCES

Some Very Common Situations

Let's do a quick summary of what we know and look at a few common situations where you may want to hypnotize him, and one where you shouldn't.

Conversational Hypnosis Summary

Total Absorption + Narrow Focus = Trance

Many Magical Moments + Time to Think = Love

Is he in trance now?

Is it a useful trance?

Do I need to induce trance? Ask childhood or other trance question, describe experience with metaphor or emotion, use TV or other free induction, retrigger previous trance with word or anchor.

What to do with trance:

Amplify nice trances and link to you.

Shift the trance: "That reminds me..." and use the trance, only limited by your

143

Craig Rovinsky

imagination (What do you want him to feel? What are your tools, (quotes, dreams, etc.)?) Here is where you personalize the trances to the unique man in front of you.

Induce a nested trance.

Adapt what you know to the current situation. That is the point of this chapter.

All the techniques in this chapter are based on the principles you have learned so far. Only the application is different. Understand what is happening in his mind in each situation. You will then be able to adapt to whatever you may run into.

You Want To Ask Him Out

Heidi came to me and during a palm reading asked if I had any suggestions about how she should ask a guy out that she was interested in. My first suggestion was simply tell him you think he is interesting and would he like to have coffee now?

Heidi understood that sounds good on paper, but was a little concerned about actually doing it. It required an emotional risk she wasn't comfortable with. We had talked about the things in Love Trances before and Heidi wanted to stack the odds in

LOVE TRANCES

her favor. She wanted my input, but after a little talking we decided this was something she should create herself. Here is how she described it to me:

Bob and I had a class together. I had accidentally seen his schedule and knew when he may be available. After class I managed to walk beside him between buildings. We talked about class and then I saw something I could use.

I asked him to stop so we could watch this squirrel. The squirrel had dug so deep into the ground for something he had only his back feet and tail sticking out. It was a fat squirrel with a real fat butt and a tail that couldn't stop frantically moving. All that was sticking out was the butt and tail, and looked hilarious.

When we thought it couldn't get better, the squirrel retrieves the nut he found, goes two feet away, quickly reburies it and scampers away.

It was while laughing at that I said to him, "I go for coffee at three. I have a real nice break. Would you like to join me?"

He replied immediately, "Yes." He was still laughing and had a twinkle in his eye.

That is what Heidi told me happened. The coffee break conversation was standard stuff you already know, occasion/location, occupation, where did you grow up, conversation 101 stuff. As you now know, if you've tried it, basic conversational trance is

145

Craig Rovinsky

very effective. Heidi and Bob now have coffee twice a week, and see each other more regularly.

Heidi had prepared the times and the coffee shop. She had already decided how she was going to ask, by describing it as something she was doing anyway. Heidi also knew she wanted him in the best trance possible. Her original idea, she told me, was just to comment on anything external to the two of them. She was going to wait for a smile, then ask.

Obviously the squirrel had his own ideas. Heidi remembered to ask on the downside of the laugh, and the result is they are both happy.

He is Just Friends and You Want More

Sarah was another client who had her eyes on one particular friend. His name was Dave. They were in the same group that hung around together, but he had never looked at her as more than a friend. Being in the same group she had some level of rapport, and this is what she did with it.

They were alone together for a few minutes as the others came and went. Sarah decided to go for it.

"I was reading an interesting article in Cosmo about sex. Do you want to hear about it?"

LOVE TRANCES

"Sure," he said (like there was any chance of a no there.)

"It said one of the strongest sexual memories we have is our first kiss. Do you remember yours?"

He was quiet for a moment. Sarah said you could see him trance out as he re-experienced the memory. After a second, with him still tranced, she asked, "What was it like?"

He started talking, but Sarah could see he was a little dreamy. "It was a summer night. We both were walking down a two-rut road. I had no idea what I was doing so when I kissed her, I pressed pretty hard. After a gentle rebuke further explorations went on into the night. It wasn't anything wilder than two teenagers kissing for the first time, but when I remember it I do smile."

"What makes you smile?" Sarah asked.

He was quiet again. "It really was a starry night in the forest. It seemed magical, surrounded by giant pine trees that vanished into the night sky. It was like a dream actually coming true. I remember feeling amazed that such a wonderful thing could happen to me."

Sarah looked at him. "Doesn't tonight seem kind of starry and magical, too?" At that point Sarah said that leaning in and kissing each other seemed the most natural thing in the world. Sarah and Dave are now a couple.

Craig Rovinsky

Sarah had planned the "I was reading an interesting article," and the subject. She originally had planned to take Dave on a three-deep exploration into his first kiss, but she never had to go that far. Once she expanded on the words "starry" and "magical" everything just clicked. She was fortunate that he had an anchor to the stars for the first kiss.

If she had to go farther she might have said, "A starry and magical night...?" and paused. With a questioning, upward inflection on the last word it is an open-ended question using his trance words and taking him deeper. Obviously this could be repeated, but usually three-deep is the maximum for effectiveness. On the other hand, if you get the result you want with one use of his trance words, you are done with that induction!

You Want To Inoculate Against Him Cheating On You

This is different than when you already suspect him cheating on you. One thing I have noticed as a palm reader is when a man suspects a woman of cheating, he is usually wrong. When a woman suspects a man of cheating, it is often worth looking into. If you suspect him of cheating on you, use the concept of nested trance from earlier in the book.

LOVE TRANCES

However, if you want to just stack the odds in your favor, I can do no better than tell you what Lisa came up with.

She had prepared what she was going to do when she had him in trance. She was wondering what the best time to induce trance would be when life gave it to her on a silver platter.

Have you ever seen an infomercial? You know the product probably doesn't work, you know the price is insane, you know the audience is all hired actors, and still you watch (and buy)! Good infomercials also have another benefit. They do multiple inductions.

You will watch and get swept along in the audience participation, the excitement will build, and the peak will come as they are offering you the chance to buy. Then, they relax and start the loop all over again. A thirty-minute kitchen-gadget infomercial will typically have three to four of these hypnotic loops in a half hour.

Lisa recognized the pattern. She watched as her boyfriend, Adam, became entranced. She saw him getting into the infomercial. When the pitch came, his interest broke. They started the next loop and she noticed him going in again. She acted.

Just before the second loop was over they looked at each other. It was the kind of look couples can give. This look meant, "Maybe that really is a cool gadget we should get." With trance and that connection moment

149

Craig Rovinsky

Lisa asked Adam, "I need your advice on something." And she muted the TV and paused for just a moment...

"I saw a talk show the other day. As usual on these shows everyone was cheating with someone else. What do guys think of other guys who cheat?"

Adam thought for a moment. "They're dogs."

"Dogs? What do you mean?"

"Dirty stinking dogs will do anything at anytime, just for themselves."

"You mean they are that selfish? You know Adam, I was never able to put it into words before, but that is why I like you and all your friends like you. You are not a dirty, stinking dog."

She was careful not to touch him during this time. It was now time to switch to positive. Lisa said to Adam, "Let's get that feeling of those dirty, stinking dogs out of us...you want to do something fun and silly?" She leaned in and whispered in his ear, "Let's order this thing!"

He looked at her and laughed. She squeezed his hand and picked up the phone. They are still together and can now use their kitchen knife to slice, dice, and make mounds of coleslaw.

This is kind of a risky induction. Any time you go to the negative you have to be careful he does not associate that with you. She stayed distant, triggered disgust for cheating

LOVE TRANCES

by driving him into his trance words, then went back to positive and anchored that to her (a whisper in the ear is always strong.)

It doesn't guarantee he won't ever cheat, but it does help. If he does manage to cheat he will feel just like that dirty, disgusting dog. (My apology to dogs everywhere. Both my wife and I love dogs (especially Wallis) but that's how she told me the story.)

I've learned you can make a mistake and the world doesn't end.
Lisa Kudrow

He Only Wants Sex

There is very little chance this could turn into anything positive. You may be interested in him as a person, but if it is obvious he wants just sex, then he very probably is in the undateable category. There may by things you can do, but at this time in his life he is too defective, at least as far as monogamous relationships go. Run, don't walk away.

The next time you run into this situation look on it as a chance to stand up for yourself. When you do, it increases your personal power. That kind of confident power is a strong attraction to men. Remember the attitude, "Is he good enough for me?" When you have a male slut on your hands is a good time to start asking yourself this question.

Craig Rovinsky

What you need to know from this chapter

There are many very common situations you can prepare for, without knowing where you will use it next.

If you just need a small agreement to move forward, laughter is a good choice for trance.

The opportunity to stand up to someone is a step toward your emotional independence.

Hypnotic Homework

The next time some greasy creep comes up to you, stand up for yourself. If you look at him and know the answer to, "Is he good enough for me?" is "no" then gently get rid of him. Then spend a few minutes, thinking of what it means for you to control your own personal self-worth.

LOVE TRANCES

HypnoJournal

Craig Rovinsky

LOVE TRANCES

The Alpha Male Trance

There probably isn't one thing alone that can make a man fall in love with you. However, a little-known male drive exists that is even more powerful than his sex drive! It's something some men and most women have no idea exists. It is:

The Alpha Male Trance

What is the alpha male trance? Well, at its core, the alpha male trance is what makes a male in a pack of dogs want to be the top dog. It's more than sex or reproduction, though those things clearly are a large component.

It is hardwired into us very, very deeply. A man who no longer cares about sex will still care about getting beat in a game.

The next time you see an ad for "male enhancement" you may be surprised to see there are very few women in the ads. Every ad I have seen is at least half of guys playing a sport, usually golf. By some miracle, the guy with the enhancement drug wins.

Logically this makes no sense. If the enhancement drug were actually working during the golf game, he probably would have a stiff putter. Not good for the driving range at all.

Craig Rovinsky

But the ad talks to men on a biological level. Being an alpha male is both sex and winning. They are very easy drives to get cross-wired and the advertisers know and use this.

For all practical purposes all males have this trance. These alpha male needs must be satisfied, must be fulfilled. There has to be something in every man's life where he feels he is the alpha male. There are many, many ways this is done.

One very common way is sports. Participation is obvious, but not so obvious is the degree of identification with a sports team. Think of how women can fantasize love, losing themselves in romance novels. Men do the same thing, becoming so involved they get the emotions of winning by watching sports. In a way, the romance novel trance and the sports trance are the same trance.

Other ways might not be so obvious. I have a friend who satisfied his needs through fantasy and comics. A video game could do it. Making money is common. Chess or crossword competitions might do it. Fixing cars or riding motorcycles can meet that need.

Have you ever talked with a guy who relives the same sports memory over and over? Maybe it was a play he made in a high school sport, a memory that has grown through the ages. Watch him go into deep

LOVE TRANCES

trance when he relives those memories. Listen to him carefully for powerful trance words and phrases.

The need is for competition/power. It might sound a little crude to put it that way, but being an alpha male is as important to most men as romance is to most women.

Other ways can be destructive. Spouse abuse, alcohol, and cheating can be ways men who feel like the bottom dog try to feel better.

> The Way a Man Satisfies His Alpha Male Needs is Critical to Your Relationship Hopes

You absolutely have to find how he satisfies his alpha male needs. If you cannot stand how he satisfies his alpha male trance, or do not like what you would need to do to be associated with it, consider it a dealbreaker. With work, such relationships can happen, but you will be unhappy with a very large part of who he is. Usually, the way a man satisfies his alpha male isn't real changeable.

You can access and associate the alpha male trance with any of the trance tools we talked about. The easiest way is to just ask him, "What do you excel at?"

157

Craig Rovinsky

You've probably noticed from the examples the format is simple: trance, suggestion, amplify, and sometimes link to you. You adapt to what you need to do. Alpha male trances are where the big payoffs are. Become accomplished at making him feel like a "big, brutin' man" and you will have his core.

Sometimes you shouldn't get too personally involved. If he is into a video game it may not do to play it against him. You may beat him (though many video games now have two player, co-op mode to put you on the same side.) But letting him know you like what he does, or getting him a book on the game are things that can create strong trance.

If he likes to go to the garage to work on cars with the guys, let him know you love it because it makes you feel...(by now, you should have some idea of the types of things you say here). Then buy him the special wrench he wanted, the one that will make him think of you while he is satisfying his alpha male needs.

It may sound too obvious, but if a man feels the woman he is with really desires <u>him</u> sexually, that accesses the alpha male trance, too.

However, don't make the mistake of making sex your primary alpha male tool. Too many women will do that. It should just be the frosting, for most men it is very

LOVE TRANCES

necessary frosting, but the real work on his alpha male trances should take place in a way only you can do. When it takes place in his heart, he is yours.

> Nothing else will bond him to you as deeply as his associating you with his alpha male feelings.

Though childhood memories are the fastest way to deep connections, the most powerful is fulfilling his alpha male needs. Save this knowledge for when you really want it. You will become the woman every man wants.

Three Things You Need to Know Before Committing

1. What is his alpha male trance?
2. Is he a cheater/beater? (Use nested trance.)
3. What is his relationship with his mother? I know this isn't trance work, but it often reflects on how he treats women.

Craig Rovinsky

One Question You Should Ask Yourself Before Committing

Is he good enough for me?

LOVE TRANCES

What You Should Know From This Chapter

Understand what an alpha male trance is. Think about how you would access it in someone you are interested in.

Hypnotic Homework

Identify the alpha male trance in a man you are talking to. Determine for yourself if this is a trance you can live with or even enjoy. If so, consider how to use what you have learned to link yourself to his feeling like an alpha male.

Craig Rovinsky

HypnoJournal

LOVE TRANCES

Super Self-Hypnosis

Here we will discuss what goes on inside your head. It's what makes the invisible part of you that is magic come out, or blocks you in. Let me describe a woman. I'm sure you know her.

She is pretty, not model beautiful, but pretty. Still, she refuses to believe it. She is basically positive and believes the best of others while setting impossible standards for herself. She would love a relationship that is both emotionally and physically passionate.

Still, when she meets someone her own internal dialogue will begin. By the time the conversation has gone just a few minutes her internal dialogue has already sent many silent body language messages all communicating the same thing.

She doesn't feel worthy and it shows. It's her "vibes." He detects it, though he doesn't know what it is. What he does know is she is vulnerable. At that point he subconsciously makes the decision to either drop her there, or use her and drop her. Do you know someone like her?

I know another woman. She isn't so pretty. As a matter of fact she is a bit common looking and could stand to loose a few pounds by anyone's standards. Still, she has a non-stop parade of romantic opportunities. Men seem mysteriously

Craig Rovinsky

attracted to her. Her subconscious thoughts send men a very different message. What's different about her?

To understand that we need to go into who you are. For most people life is one trance state after another, morning to night. From rising awake in the morning to dropping asleep at night we drift from one trance to another. A philosopher from the early 20th century named Gurdjieff once asked, "Is there life on earth?"

Who you think you are is a collection of automatic trance behaviors that run more or less constantly. Most were developed when you were young and your mind just runs them automatically all through your life. A trance trigger happens and a program runs.

This presents a problem. Many of the behaviors and beliefs you had when you were four years old just don't work very well for an adult. These trances do not change on their own.

To change this you have two weapons. The first is self-hypnosis, just bringing yourself into a deep state where suggestions you choose can be planted. Consistently pursued this can make permanent change over a very short time.

The second weapon is modeling. Have you ever played make-believe as a kid? Ever fantasize you were someone other than yourself as an adult? Warrior, princess, romance heroine? By taking on personas

LOVE TRANCES

that already come with the personal characteristics you choose you can have instant change. I'll describe how to do each, self-hypnosis in this chapter and modeling in the next.

It's 5% talent, 15% skill, and 80% hanging in there.
Lucy Lawless

The Most Powerful Hypnotic Induction in the World.

The process of inducing a formal hypnotic trance is simple. I will teach you what I consider to be the most powerful induction. It's what I use on stage and in hypnotherapy. It has the added benefit of being so easy it can be used for self-hypnosis.

Once you have the trance state you can insert the suggestions you desire. How to word suggestions and what suggestions to use will be unique to you. There's a good chance you already have some idea what you want to accomplish. Here is the induction.

Be someplace quiet. You are going to be deeply relaxed. A phone ringing may cause you to jump straight up to the ceiling. You get my drift. You want comfy and quiet.

It's time for a stage hypnotist's secret. The muscles of the eyelids are among the weakest of the body. Locking the eyes shut in a few moments looks impressive to a

Craig Rovinsky

crowd. It also works on just about everyone and when the person being hypnotized experiences it they go deeper into trance. It's also fun to do. Most people have never experienced having their mind control their body and it's a gently empowering rush when you realize you can do mind over body.

You know you can clench your hand. You can squeeze it so hard that for all practical purposes you can't squeeze any tighter. You also know you can relax your hand until it is limp. With a little attention paid to the muscles you can decide how much to relax. You can also do this with your eyelids. Being such thin muscles, when you relax them deeply they aren't strong enough to open!

Keep in mind what you are doing. <u>You are not trying to prove you can't open your eyes. You are using your mind to relax your eyelids until they are just flaps of skin lying there</u>. When you do this relax your lids until they are loose and limp. After you have relaxed them try to open them. Just test them once or twice to see if they are so relaxed you can't open them. If you can it just means you haven't relaxed them enough.

Take it from me; I've done this thousands of time on stage. Nine out of ten get it the first time and it is neat to see their expressions when it starts to sink in that they have controlled their body with their mind. If you don't get it the first time just

LOVE TRANCES

slowly exhale, close your eyes and relax again.

Relaxation builds on itself, each time you relax it goes deeper. When you have relaxed your eyes to the point where they won't open stop trying, relax your eyes even more and enjoy the feeling for a few moments. Allow yourself to open your eyes, and repeat. After a few times it will become difficult to open your eyes at all, they are so relaxed.

This one technique is a fantastic stress-buster. Once you do this you'll be able to relax almost anywhere, anytime.

Don't ever do this driving, as you may not realize how deep you are.

The next step is simple. Now that your eyes are deeply relaxed, just leave them closed. Take that relaxation from your eyes and spread it out through your body. Let the relaxation pass down your arms and relax your hands. It flows through your body, relaxing your face and jaw and going all the way down to your toes. After you have relaxed all through your body allow yourself to open your eyes.

Immediately close your eyes again and do the relaxation cycle, eyelids first, relax until they are too limp to open, then spreading that relaxation through the body. Open your eyes, close them and repeat.

Craig Rovinsky

The repetition gives you the effect of being rehypnotized over and over, sending you deeper than you could imagine. There is no set number. Just do it a few times until you feel deeply relaxed.

Now you will relax your mind. From the eyes closed, relaxed state imagine the number 100 in your mind. It might be on a blackboard, a neon light, or a sign or just floating there, it doesn't matter. Just imagine that number and let it fade from 100 to 99. Continue to let numbers fade as they get smaller, 100, 99, 98...just gently relax them out of your mind. For most people the numbers relax away and vanish by 98 or 97. If you still have numbers at 96 or 95 just let them relax out and don't replace them.

That's it. If you do this you will be in a deep trance. At this point you can input suggestions to yourself and they will go straight to your unconscious. As I mentioned, the specific use is up to you. Nothing beats experience. If you are a reader and like to look all through a book before trying things, make a decision now to do something new. Before you go any further, stop... and do the eye relaxation. It's the difference between describing a kiss and having one.

LOVE TRANCES

A guy doesn't have to be Brad Pitt, he doesn't have to have some great car, and he doesn't have to be a rocket scientist. He just has to be there when you need him.
Shania Twain

Your Own Hypnotic Love Talisman

When in a trance you can create a powerful hypnotic talisman to give you access to the emotions you want. Bring yourself into trance, open your eyes allowing your brain to remain in that state. Now create the exact emotion or emotions you want to be able to access at will. Cosmo magazine has a motto, "fun, fearless, female." If you haven't figured out what your personal power trance words are, this is a good start. It is best if you use your personal trance words to build the state, though.

Once you've built the state you want in trance imagine a space at your "third eye" (this is the space in your forehead, just above the space between your eyes). Imagine in this space a color forming. The color is the one that matches the state you want. It may not be a single color but a kaleidoscope, but whatever you associate with the state you want is fine. If you're not sure, ask your subconscious to create the correct color.

Now imagine that color taking a shape in your third eye and moving or spinning. It could be anything from a circle to a

169

Craig Rovinsky

thousand-pointed star. This may be moving or spinning in any direction at any speed. There is no single right way. Whatever your brain creates is right for you. As you watch the color and shape spinning and moving in your imagination amplify the feeling you want.

Next, imagine the entire shape moving down to the hollow of your throat, that little notch where the neck meets the chest bone. When it gets there, amplify it again.

Now move it to your heart area amplifying it again. The color may get brighter, it may move faster...don't worry; your subconscious will make the changes.

Next come completely out of trance, go back in and repeat the heart portion until every time you imagine that personal shape and color and movement it puts you in the state you want.

Now imagine the shape without trance. If it doesn't trigger the state you want, go back into self-hypnosis and reprogram yourself until it does.

You now have a personal hypnotic talisman in your heart that allows you to feel how you want to feel whenever you want. Practice and rehearse this until it is automatic and you will have the ability to be who you want whenever you wish.

Never let anyone know your color, movement or shape. That would give them access to your heart when they want. This is

LOVE TRANCES

a way for you to feel as beautiful and deliciously wonderful whenever you wish.

Obviously, this can be used as an "imagination exercise" with someone else. Just leave out the never let anyone else know part. Still, this is most effective when you just use it for yourself. You know enough at this point to adapt it to your needs.

I am strong. I am invincible. I am woman.
Helen Reddy

Change can be rapid. Still, while teaching your mind to automatically do what you want it to, you still need love. Until your natural charisma emerges you need a way to get instant charisma. I call that method useful hallucinations.

Craig Rovinsky

What You Should Know From This Chapter

Your "vibes" come from how you feel about yourself inside.

How you feel about yourself can change with hypnosis and modeling.

The best hypnotic induction in the world consists of relaxing your eyelids until they won't open, allowing yourself to open your eyes, and repeating the eye relaxation several times. After the eyes no longer want to open allow the feeling to flow down your body. Allow yourself to open your eyes and repeat eyes closed/body relaxed several times. Finally leave your eyes closed and count down from 100, relaxing the numbers out of your mind until they vanish in the mid-nineties.

You can give yourself a gift of an invisible magic hypnotic talisman. This will allow you to feel whatever you decide you want to, whenever you want to.

Hypnotic Homework

Create your own personal hypnotic talisman. Do the work necessary so it is personally powerful. This will give you a

LOVE TRANCES

resource no one can ever take away. It is more work than creating your personal power song, but infinitely more powerful.

Craig Rovinsky

HypnoJournal

LOVE TRANCES

Useful Hallucinations

Useful hallucinations? Remember what your mind does. It takes a trance and filters the world through it. Useful trances can be created in your own mind quickly and just as strongly. Even an idiot can do this. Someone happens to come to mind...

About 25 years ago I had a friend named Celine. She was a heavy-set, slow-witted, ski-slope nosed burn out who stole a large portion of my stuff and moved to Hawaii. Did I mention that men fell all over her? She wasn't the brightest bulb in the chandelier but had a hell of a secret.

She told me that when she went to a party (nightly, I think her GPA was under 1.5 out of 4.0) she would convince herself she was a movie star. She never had anyone particular in mind but by thoroughly believing in her mind she was a movie star she acted that way on a subconscious level. Men could feel it and flocked to her. Basically she played make believe, just like a child.

I tried it a few times and found my friend had stumbled onto something. For you to use this decide that you are going to play. Pick someone you admire or would like to be. To amplify it just quickly do the eye relaxation portion of the trance and imagine you are her.

Craig Rovinsky

Just go out and play make-believe you are her. Use your own name and don't tell anyone. Watch the reactions. If one persona doesn't give you the desired results do another. Have a number of people you can become for different situations. Choosing your personality is another time you can happen to life, instead of life happening to you.

Combining your personal hallucination with believing the other person is a celebrity (silent hypnosis from earlier in the book) also creates an emotional feedback loop that must be experienced to be believed. Master imagining them as a celebrity first, as mentioned in the listening section earlier. Next learn to do it in your own head. Learn them separately before combining them and the loop will come easily to you.

Are you concerned this isn't "you?" Think about who you are, a collection of likes, fears and fantasies that imprinted in the first five years of your life and haven't changed. Try new "you's."

If you don't like them you can always go back to the five year old you. Most people aren't losing anything great. Hallucinations you do in your own mind are no different than the hallucinations you were given as a child.

LOVE TRANCES

Seeing With His Eyes

Another powerful hallucination is to step into someone else and see you through his eyes. While talking with someone imagine that you are in their mind, looking at you through their eyes. Literally imagine what they are seeing. This is nuclear-powered bonding and is as easy as reading the sentence. It forms an emotional loop between the two of you with very little effort.

The most important thing is to be whatever you are without shame.
Rod Steiger

One Trance To Eliminate

Emotional leaning is a core trance that is easily noticed and controlled once you are aware of it. Most people lean "out." Imagine the feeling that is your emotional center. Now, the next time you are seeking someone's approval notice where that center is. "Leaning" is as close as words can get but you can feel it is the opposite of being centered.

Always keep your emotional center inside of you. The less you lean the happier you will be. To your mind the emotional center moves and is real. Experiment with different feelings, locations and intensities for this center. It gives you much control for little effort.

Craig Rovinsky

There are many practical hallucinations you can choose to experience, limited only by your sense of playfulness. Still, this is about becoming the romance heroine in your life. You can choose your happiness and have the ability to teach a man to love. At its core, that is the plot of the romance novel.

Becoming a romance heroine is not about focusing on having men in your life, though. It is about you living the adventure that is your life with romantic love being just one aspect. With a bit of practice you will attract many delightful options and don't be surprised if they expand beyond romance. Then the only limit is your imagination.

I never loved another person the way I loved myself.
Mae West

LOVE TRANCES

What You Should Know From This Chapter

The trances in your mind determine your happiness. Choose the trances you want.

Modeling someone you admire can give you her major personality traits instantly.

See in your mind's eye what he is seeing in his mind, through his eyes.

Eliminate the "emotional leaning'" trance.

Hypnotic Homework

Do the "seeing through his eyes" trance. The simplicity of this technique cannot convey its impact.

Craig Rovinsky

HypnoJournal

LOVE TRANCES

Once upon a time a woman came to a palm reader. He gazed deeply into her hand and began, "You are now becoming the romance heroine you've always dreamed you could be..."

To order more copies of Love Trances for yourself or as gifts for friends go to lovetrances.com or if you prefer you can call the publisher, 1stBooks Library, to order at 1-888-280-7715.

About The Author

Craig Rovinsky has developed a unique perspective on life over the last twenty years. As a stage hypnotist and palm reader his experiences have given him a very practical outlook. Thousands of hypnotic inductions taught him how the mind works. Tens of thousands of palm readings showed him the hidden secrets of men and women. In *LOVE TRANCES*, he shares his knowledge to answer the question women ask most... "How do I find love?"

Milton Keynes UK
Ingram Content Group UK Ltd.
UKHW011312031023
429868UK00001B/18